Old Bergen [NJ]

History and Reminiscences

Daniel Van Winkle

HERITAGE BOOKS
2019

HERITAGE BOOKS
AN IMPRINT OF HERITAGE BOOKS, INC.

Books, CDs, and more—Worldwide

For our listing of thousands of titles see our website
at
www.HeritageBooks.com

A Facsimile Reprint
Published 2019 by
HERITAGE BOOKS, INC.
Publishing Division
5810 Ruatan Street
Berwyn Heights, Md. 20740

Copyright © 1902 Daniel Van Winkle

— Publisher's Notice —
In reprints such as this, it is often not possible to remove blemishes from the original. We feel the contents of this book warrant its reissue despite these blemishes and hope you will agree and read it with pleasure.

International Standard Book Number
Paperbound: 978-0-7884-0694-2

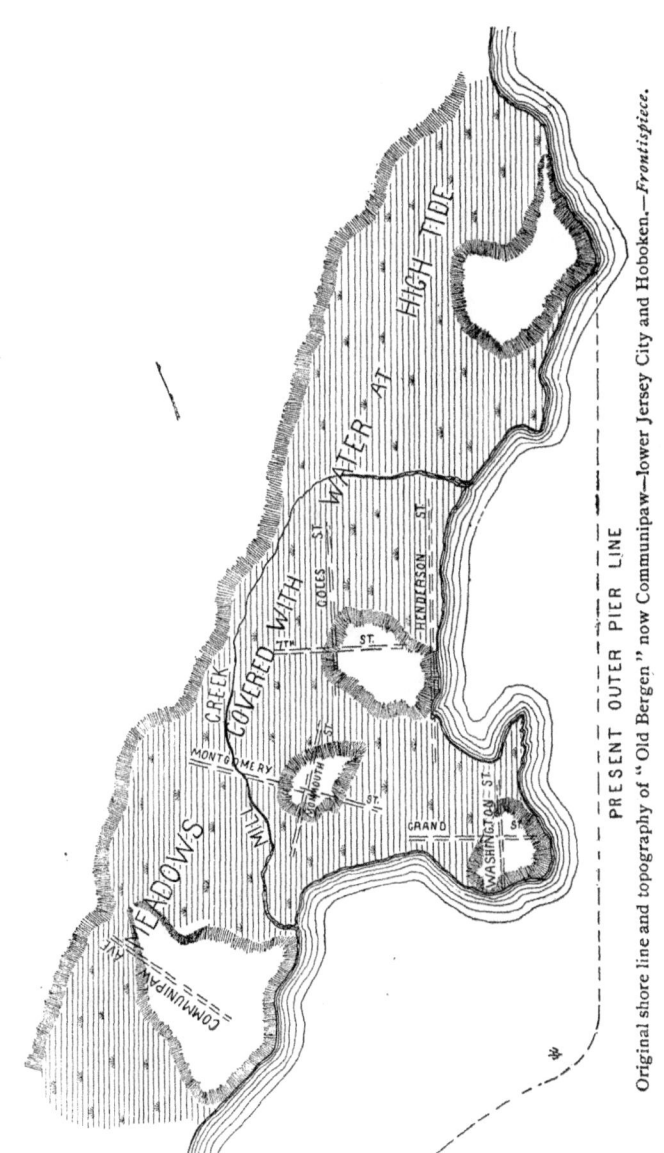

Original shore line and topography of "Old Bergen" now Communipaw—lower Jersey City and Hoboken.—*Frontispiece.*

Preface.

This little volume is projected with the hope of exciting a new interest in the territory of which it treats.

From its antiquity and historical importance, "Old Bergen" deserves more than a passing glance. Founded during the infancy of our country, and standing at the gateway of the continent, it was subjected during the colonial and revolutionary period to the privations and vicissitudes peculiar to those early days, to an unusual degree. Although located under the shadow of a great city, its bosom seamed and scarred by the ebb and flow of the traffic and commerce of the Great West, it preserved until very recent years the customs and conditions of "The Long Ago."

The people inhabiting its territory, retaining to a great extent the characteristics and conservativeness of their forefathers, were oftentimes visited by their city neighbors, when tired and worn with the cares and anxieties of a business life, to secure a momentary relaxation and rest among their peaceful surroundings.

Although by no means exhaustive, the matter presented in this book is reliable and authentic. It has been procured from all available sources and carefully selected : The historical facts, from colonial records and revolutionary documents; libraries have been freely consulted, and files of old newspapers scanned in search of matters of local interest, while the traditions and reminiscences indulged in from time to time, have been gathered through a succession of generations, and many of t em here rescued from that oblivion into which so many have fallen.

A few generations ago, much unquestionable traditionary information could have been secured, but owing to the lapse of time, traditions have been forgotten and documents destroyed, that might have aided us greatly in our search for information affecting the homes and people of "Old Bergen." Through the general growth of our country and changed conditions, "Old Bergen" has been absorbed by the greater Jersey City, and lost its identity in its new relations. With the hope of rescuing its name from oblivion, and that other investigations may be continued, to secure more fully, whatever there may be of existing data relating to the "Olden Days," this volume is issued.

DANIEL VAN WINKLE.

Bergen (Jersey City Heights), January, 1902.

TABLE OF CONTENTS.

CHAPTER I.
INTRODUCTION—EARLY TRADE CONDITIONS, . . 1-3

CHAPTER II.
DISCOVERY OF THE REGION OF THE HUDSON, . . 4-8

CHAPTER III.
CLAIMS OF EARLY DISCOVERERS AND INDIAN LEGENDS, 9-14

CHAPTERS IV AND V.
SETTLEMENT OF NEW NETHERLANDS, ... 15-22

CHAPTER VI.
DIFFICULTIES ENCOUNTERED, ... 23-25

CHAPTERS VII AND VIII.
SETTLEMENT OF "OLD BERGEN," 26-32

CHAPTER IX.
THE NATIVE INHABITANTS, ... 33-36

CHAPTER X.
DISSATISFACTION WITH GOV. KIEFT AND RESULTS, . 37-41

CHAPTER XI.
CONTINUANCE OF INDIAN TROUBLES, . . . 42-46

CHAPTER XII.
PRECAUTIONARY MEASURES ADOPTED, . . . 47-51

CHAPTERS XIII-XIV AND XV.
BERGEN, ... 52-66

CHAPTER XVI.
CURRENCY AND CAPTURE BY ENGLAND, . . . 67-72

CONTENTS.

CHAPTER XVII.
Bergen Becomes an English Colony, . . . 73-75

CHAPTER XVIII.
Bergen Becomes again a Dutch Dependency, . 76-78

CHAPTERS XIX and XX.
Growth of Bergen, ... 79-90

CHAPTERS XXI—XXX.
Revolutionary Times, ... 91-139

CHAPTER XXXI.
Close of the Revolution, ... 140-144

CHAPTER XXXII.
Growth and Characteristics, ... 145-147

CHAPTER XXXIII.
Changes, ... 148-154

CHAPTER XXXIV.
Transportation, ... 155-162

CHAPTER XXXV.
Church and School, ... 163-170

CHAPTERS XXXVI and XXXVII.
Church, ... 171-180

CHAPTER XXXVIII.
Later History of Church, ... 181-185

CHAPTER XXXIX.
Church Customs, ... 186-191

CHAPTER XL.
The Church, ... 192-194

CHAPTER XLI.
Other Churches, ... 195-202

CHAPTER XLII.
Schools, ... 203-210

CONTENTS.

CHAPTER XLIII.
COLUMBIAN ACADEMY, ... 211–216

CHAPTER XLIV.
OTHER EARLY SCHOOL ACCOMMODATIONS, . . 217–222

CHAPTERS XLV AND XLVI.
GROWTH AND CHANGES OF "OLD BERGEN," . . 223–235

CHAPTER XLVII.
CHARACTERISTICS OF INHABITANTS, . . . 236–240

CHAPTER XLVIII.
WARS OF 1812 AND 1861 AND OLD LANDMARKS, . 241–252

CHAPTER XLIX.
CHANGES AND OLD LANDMARKS CONTINUED, . . 253–262

CHAPTER L.
CHANGES, ... 263–273

CHAPTER LI.
HOBOKEN, ... 274–280

CHAPTER LII.
HOBOKEN AND TRADITION, ... 281–289

CHAPTERS LIII–LIV AND LV.
TRADITIONS AND REMINISCENCES, ... 290–306

CHAPTER LVI.
CUSTOMS AND HABITS, , ⋅ 307–311

CHAPTER LVII.
THE OLD HOMES, ... 312–316

CHAPTER LVIII.
CUSTOMS, ... 317–319

ILLUSTRATIONS.

Original Shore Line and Topography	*Frontispiece*
Henry Hudson	4
Half-Moon	6
Van Vorst's Bouerie	27
Mill Creek	39
Map of Bergen	56
Communipaw	61
Fort at Paulus Hook	93
Map John Champe's Route	119
Line Lee's Retreat	131
Race Between Horse Car and "Tom Thumb"	152
Grasshopper Engine	160
Octagonal Church	166
Doctor Dubois	170
Old Church	173
Old Parsonage	177
Doctor Taylor	182
Present Church	183
Doctor Amerman	184
Doctor Brett	185
Columbian Academy	213
Geo. H. Linsley	220
W. L. Dickinson	221
Old Ferry	231
Old Well	246
Edge's Windmill	254
Prior's Mill	258
Thatched Cottage	261
Old Tavern	267
Weehawken Duelling Ground	285
Weehawken Duelling Ground (Present)	287
Cider Mill	302
Old Home	313

"Haec olim meminisse juvabit."

Chapter I.

INTRODUCTION.

THE strife for commercial supremacy among the nations of the Old World, in the latter part of the fifteenth and the beginning of the sixteenth centuries, produced far-reaching results. The mercantile rivalry of the times engendered a spirit of enterprise that resulted in the discovery of a new continent, and the development of a new world.

The difficulties and dangers attending the trade with India, China and Japan, as carried on through the Mediterranean and by the overland route to the Persian Gulf and Red Sea, were so great that the merchants of the day put forth every effort to discover some plan whereby the tediousness and expense of such voyages could be avoided. Expeditions were fitted out to ascertain whether India might not be reached by skirting the coast of Africa, and several attempts were made in this direction. These expeditions proceeded cautiously, pushing to the south, each one somewhat farther than the preceding one, until Vasco De Gama, in the year 1497, succeeded in rounding the southernmost point of Africa and reached the eastern coast of Asia.

Meanwhile the belief had grown that the Far East could be reached by sailing due west, and the attention of all navigators was turned in this direction. The sagas of the Northmen which told of lands reached in the dim past by sailing in a westerly direction, were corroborated, at least in theory, by the investigations of mariners who gave special thought to the problems of the unknown sea.

At last Columbus, braving the dangers of the "Sea of Darkness" (as the Atlantic was called), which according to the ignorance and superstition of the times was filled with all imaginable horrors and peopled with hideous monsters, proved that such dangers were but imaginary. He determined the correctness of his theory, that the form of the earth was spherical, by sailing westward and reaching, as he thought, the eastern coast of India.

On his return to Spain with evidences of his discovery, new interest was excited, his theory was generally accepted, and his glowing reports stimulated anew the spirit of commercial enterprise. Nations vied with each other in sending expeditions to the west, and the seas which had been regarded with so much terror were now looked upon as affording new opportunities for enlargement of territory, and the development of that wealth and power so eagerly sought after.

According to the laws of the times, any new territory discovered by any navigator became the property of the nation under whose flag he sailed; and the opportunities for the acquisition of new territory and the resultant benefits therefrom, as presented by the report of Columbus, produced the most energetic efforts to secure these advantages. Among those who pursued the search in quest of a direct route to the East were John and Sebastian Cabot, who demonstrated that the prevailing idea, that the land discovered was part of the eastern coast of India, was erroneous; and by their continued explorations they determined the existence of a great continent. The desire to secure the advantages offered by these discoveries was general, and settlements were projected by the different nations on the shores of the New World.

While England was establishing her first permanent settlements in America, and France was following the great rivers and lakes into the interior at the north; and while Spain, her cupidity excited by the tales of fabulous riches, was pushing her explorations in search of the coveted gold throughout the extreme south; the Netherlands had revolted against Spanish rule and established the Dutch Republic. They drove the Spanish and Portuguese from the ocean and built up a trade with India and the East. Companies were formed by their merchants, the better to prosecute their trade; one of which was the East India Company. Eager to secure any trade advantage, and desirous of avoiding the long and tedious voyage around the Cape of Good Hope, this company determined to search for a more direct route to the Indies; and they accordingly secured the services of Henry Hudson, an experienced navigator, to prosecute this search.

Chapter II.

DISCOVERY OF THE REGION OF THE HUDSON.

WITH a crew of sixteen men, Englishmen and Hollanders, Hudson set sail from the Texel on April 6, 1609, directing his course toward the north. He arrived at Newfoundland, and, sailing along the coast in a southwesterly direction, reached Delaware Bay; whence returning and skirting the easterly shore of New Jersey, on Sept. 3, 1609, he discovered, as he thought, the long-sought-for passage. The next morning he passed within Sandy Hook and there anchored, determining to continue his explorations on the following day. His experiences are related in the following extracts from his Report:

HENRY HUDSON.

"During the night a storm arose, and the wind blowing from the northeast, the vessel was driven on shore, but as the ground was soft sand and ooze, it was not harmed. . . . The people of the country came aboard of us, seeming very glad of our coming, and brought green tobacco and gave of it for knives and beads. . . . In the morning as soon as the day was light, the wind ceased and the flood came, so we heaved off our ship again in five fathoms of water. Some of the Indians came aboard of the vessel, but at night they were sent on shore as they were not to be trusted."

He decided, however, to continue his voyage, and on the sixth of September he made preparations to ascend the passage. He passed through the Narrows, and sent in a boat's crew to investigate. Sailing along the shore of Staten Island, they passed through the Kill von Kull and entered Newark Bay ; but finding that the sought-for passage was evidently not in that direction, they retraced their route. While returning through the Kills, they were attacked by the Indians and one of the crew killed. The remainder reached the vessel in safety, bearing the dead body of their companion.

The Indians now showed such an unfriendly disposition that a strict watch was maintained to guard against treachery. Determining from the investigations of the crew that the desired passage lay before him, Hudson weighed anchor, and from the 7th to the 13th the vessel slowly and cautiously worked its way through the bay to about Weehawken Cove, where he again anchored.

We can scarcely appreciate the emotions of this bold navigator who, after many years of searching and stormy buffetings, found himself, as he supposed, on the threshold of a discovery that would revolutionize the trade of the then known world. Standing on the

THE HALF-MOON.

deck of his vessel on that autumnal morning, his eyes rested upon the fairest picture that ever sun shone upon. As he passed through the Narrows, he saw stretching out before him the glittering road that was to lead to fame and fortune. Surrounded by the wooded hills of Long and Staten Islands, with the rocky shores of New Jersey rising in the distance, the magnificent bay and river reached off to the northeast, as if beckoning him on to the long-sought-for goal.

On the arrival of the vessel at Weehawken Cove, it was surrounded by the canoes of Indians from the west bank, who desired to trade with the white strangers. They seemed peaceably inclined and friendly. Hudson says: "They go in deer-skins, loose and well dressed; they desire clothes and are civil; those from the east side were more fierce, while those from the west side, while we lay at anchor, brought for barter the largest and finest oysters, Indian corn and vegetables."

The next morning, the 14th, Hudson commenced ascending the stream, but he soon discovered, from the shallowing of the water, that he had not succeeded in finding the northwest passage. He continued his investigations, however, reaching a point above Albany on the 23rd. Jouet states: "Higher up it becomes so shallow that small skiffs can with difficulty sail there, and one sees in the distance several lofty hills from whence most of the water in the river flows."

Returning thence, Hudson explored the adjoining country and traded with the Indians for skins of wild beasts and products of the soil. He reached Weehawken Cove and again anchored there on the 2nd of October. Jouet says: "Within a while after, we got down about two leagues beyond that place " (Haverstraw Bay), " and anchored in a Bay clear from all danger on the other side of the River. We here saw a good piece of ground, and hard by there was a cliff " (Castle Point) " that looked of the color of white green, as though it was either a copper or silver mine, and I think it to be one of these by the trees that grow upon it, for they are all burned and the other places are green grass. . . . There we saw no people to trouble us and rode quietly all night, but had much wind and rain. The 3rd was very stormy, and in the morning in a gust of wind and rain we drove on the ground, but it was oozy. We had much wind and rain, with thick weather, so we rode all night. The 4th being fair weather, we weighed anchor and came out of the great mouth of the great river that runneth to the northwest " (junction of Hackensack and Passaic Rivers), " and by 12 o'clock we were clear of the inlet. On the 5th we continued our course toward England without seeing any land by the way." It is thus seen that Hudson left the harbor through the Kills, and passing around Staten Island, reached the ocean.

Although Hudson had failed in his endeavor to secure a short passage to the East, the knowledge that he had discovered a country of such boundless resources, doubtless reconciled him to his want of success.

Chapter III.

DISCOVERY OF THE HUDSON REGION, AND INDIAN LEGENDS.

ALTHOUGH various discoveries had from time to time brought into notice different parts of the New World, we have no positive proof of any discovery of the Hudson River and the region in its immediate vicinity, before this memorable voyage of Hudson in 1609. Claims of prior discoveries have been made, but the fact remains that none resulted in any practical benefit, previous to the discovery of Hudson.

Some assert that the Cabots, in their earlier voyages, discovered this territory, yet although they sailed along the coast from Labrador to Virginia, they do not mention any particular bay or river, which they probably would have done had they entered and explored our own magnificent bay and harbor. Verrazano, in his account of his voyage in 1524, gives a general description which might be applied to this territory, but the details are not given with sufficient exactness to verify any such claim. Tradition states that some Dutch in the employ of the Greenland Whale Company came into the bay for winter quarters, and built a fort for temporary protection, in 1598.

Notwithstanding these claims, Adrien Vander

Donk, who wrote in 1650, states as follows: "That this country was first found and discovered by the Netherlanders, is evident and clear from the fact that the Indians, or natives of the land, many of whom are still living, and with whom I have conversed, declared freely that before the arrival of the Lowland ship, the *Half-Moon,* in the year 1609, they (the natives) did not know that there were any other people in the world than those who were like themselves, much less any people who differed so much in appearance from them as we did. Some of them supposed the ship to be a strange fish or monster."

Lambrechtsen says that "John and Sebastian Cabot, while seeking a passage through the Northwest, probably did *see* the shores of America, although they did not visit them;" and Robertson asserts that "The Hollanders, having discovered the island of Manhattan with the districts along its shores, acquired all the rights to these which can be given by first possession." Hudson's Report of his voyage, and his description of country discovered by him, justify the claim that the territory of the Hudson was first opened up by him under the auspices of the Netherlanders.

As an item of interest the following legend, bearing somewhat on the discovery of the Hudson, is here inserted. It is interesting because it alludes to events that occurred at different times, which are mingled without any regard to chronological happenings, having been handed down through the traditions and legends of the different tribes. Rev. John Heckewelder, for many years a Moravian missionary to the Indians in Pennsylvania, states in a letter dated January 26, 1801, as follows:—

"I received my information from Indians in their language and style. I return it in the same way. A long time ago when there was no such thing known to the Indians, as people with white skin, some Indians who had been out a-fishing, and where the sea widens, espied at a great distance something remarkably large, swimming, or floating on the water, and such as they had never seen before. They, immediately returning to the shore, apprised their countrymen of what they had seen, and pressed them to go out with them, and discover what it might be. These together hurried out, and saw to their great surprise the phenomenon, but could not agree what it might be; some concluding it either to be an uncommon large fish, or other animal, while others were of the opinion, it must be some very large house.

"It was at length agreed among those who were spectators, that this phenomenon moved toward the land; whether or not it was an animal, or anything that had life in it, it would be well to inform all the Indians on the inhabited islands of what they had seen, and put them on their guard. Accordingly, they sent runners and watermen off, to carry the news to their scattered chiefs, that these might send off in every direction, for the warriors to come in. These arriving in numbers, and themselves viewing the strange appearance, and that it was actually moving towards them (the entrance of the River or Bay), concluded it to be a large canoe, or house, in which the great Manitou (Supreme Being) himself was, and that he probably was coming to visit them.

"By this time the chiefs of the different tribes were assembled on York Island, and were counselling on the manner they should receive their Manitou on his arrival—fresh runners arrive, declaring it a house of many colors, and crowded with living creatures—other runners soon after arriving, declare it a large house of various colors, full of people, yet of quite a different color than they (the Indians)—many are for running off to the woods, but are pressed by others to stay, in order not to give offense to their visitors, who could find them out and might destroy them.

"The house (or large canoe as some will have it) stops, and a smaller canoe comes ashore. Some stay by this canoe to guard it. The chiefs and wise men had composed a circle, unto which the red-clothed man, with two others approach. He salutes them with friendly countenance, and they return the salute after their manner. They think he must be the great Manitou, but why should he have a white skin?

"A large hock hack (bottle) is brought forward by one of his servants, and from this a substance is poured out, in a small cup, and handed to the Manitou. He drinks, and has the glass filled again, and hands it to the chief next to him to drink. He only smelleth at it, and passes it on to the next chief, who does likewise. The glass thus passes through the circle, without the contents being tasted by anyone, and is on the point of being returned . . . when one of their number said it was given to them to be drank, and if no one was willing to drink it, he would. He then took the glass and drank it off. He soon began staggering about, and dropping to the ground, fell into a deep sleep. He awakes again, jumps up, and declares that he never felt himself before so happy. He wishes for more, and the whole assembly soon join, and become intoxicated.

"After this general intoxication had ceased, the man with the red clothes came again to them (from the vessel), and distributed presents of beads, axes, hoes, stockings, etc. They say they had become familiar to each other and were made to understand by signs. . . . The white men said they now would return home, but would visit them next year again, when they would bring them more presents, and stay with them awhile, but that they could not live without eating, and would want a little land to plant.

"That the vessel arrived the season following, and they were much rejoiced at seeing each other, but the whites laughed at them, as they used the axes and hoes hanging to their breasts as ornaments, and the stockings for tobacco pouches. The whites now showed them the use of these, and a great laughter ensued because they, the Indians, had remained so long ignorant of such valuable implements. . . . Familiarity increasing between them and the whites, the latter now propose to stay with them, asking them for only so much land as the hide of a bullock would cover, which hide was brought forward and spread on the ground before them.

"That they readily granted this request; whereupon the whites took a knife and beginning at one place on this hide, cut it up into a rope not thicker than the finger of a little child, so that by the time this hide was cut up, there was a great heap. That this rope was drawn out to a great distance, and then brought round again, so that both ends might meet. That they carefully encompassed a large piece of ground. . . . That they and the whites lived for a long time contentedly together, although they asked from time to time, for more land of them ; and proceeding higher up the Mahicanituck (Hudson) River, they believed they would want all their country, which was at this time, already the case."

Chapter IV.

SETTLEMENT OF NEW NETHERLANDS.

ALTHOUGH the East India Company did not take any immediate steps to develop or occupy the territory discovered by Hudson, some of the merchants of Amsterdam, feeling that a hitherto unknown country had been opened up to the mercantile world that bade fair to rival even the Indies in the magnitude of its commercial possibilities, became deeply interested.

Hudson's Report stated that he found the soil fruitful, the rivers teeming with fish, and the immeasurable forests and numerous swamps the abode of wild beasts, whose skins were greatly valued as articles of trade; in short, "that it was the most beautiful country on which you could tread with your feet. . . . The natives are good natured and the climate very nearly to ours."

This favorable account of the country aroused their enthusiasm to such an extent that, in the following year, 1610, they freighted a vessel with a variety of goods suitable for traffic with the native tribes that dwelt about the Hudson River and its vicinity. On its arrival, so great was their encouragement that a trading post was established on Manhattan Island, to facilitate trade with the Indians occupying the country round about.

In 1613, Capt. Samuel Argalls, returning to Virginia from his expedition against Acadia, discovered the small settlement of Dutch merchants on Manhattan Island—as he reported, " four houses built, and a pretended Dutch Governor under the West India Company of Amsterdam, share or part, who kept trading boats and trucking with the Indians." He claimed the ownership of the whole territory for His Majesty of England " as part of Virginia." Hendrick Christaen, who was the *opperkoopman*, or superintendent of trade on the river, submitted to this asserted authority.

After the departure of Argalls, the Dutch merchants sent information to Holland of his interference, and Christaen was removed and a new superintendent sent over. The latter not only refused to pay tribute, but erected forts and " put himself in a posture of defence," and it is added " that the claim of the English being either wholly waived for the present, or but faintly pursued, they " (the Dutch) "the same year, made a firm settlement, which soon became very flourishing and populous." Fort Amsterdam was then erected, near the ground now known as the Battery, on the southern extremity of Manhattan Island.

To encourage trade, the States General issued an edict March 27, 1614, by which, " all and every, of the inhabitants who should discover any courses, havens, countries or places, should have the right to frequent them for four voyages." Under this edict five ships were fitted out by a number of merchants, and despatched under the direction of Adrian Block, Hendrick Cortstiansen and Cornelius Jacobus May. They established small trading-posts, and from them small vessels explored the neighboring bays and creeks. The prospect of trade with the new territory being encouraging, the early pioneers united themselves into a trading company, and made application to the States General for a charter which would give them a monopoly of traffic in that region. This was granted under the name of the United New Netherlands Company, October 11, 1614, and the unoccupied region of America lying between Virginia and Canada, was designated as the New Netherlands. They thus became possessed of the right to trade exclusively in this territory, including the region along the Hudson. They at once despatched vessels suitably laden for the purpose of trading with the Indians, and built forts and established trading posts at New Amsterdam and up the Hudson.

Block and May appear to have returned shortly after to Holland, to render an account of their discoveries, and obtain if possible the privilege of exclusive trade. Christansen, who remained in this country, determined to secure any advantage that might be obtained. He went up the Hudson and erected a rude fortification on an island near the west bank below Albany, which was called Fort Orange; and leaving some of the company here, he returned with the remainder to Fort Amsterdam, which, as stated, was situated near the mouth of the river on the Island of Manhattan.

It must be remembered that these early settlements were the result of *private* enterprise, and instituted by a *private* corporation, organized under the auspices of the home government, but only nominally protected by it. The Company's headquarters was established at New Amsterdam, and the records relating to the territory were kept there. These early records related mostly to trading operations in general, and consequently detailed accounts concerning any particular territory are not to be found. It is safe to assume, however, that the territory on the west bank of the Hudson opposite the trading center, was just as important in its relation to the traffic of that day as it is at present, when the bulk of the wealth of this vast country is poured out at its wharves.

Chapter V.

SETTLEMENT OF NEW NETHERLANDS CONTINUED.

IN the spring of 1623, the first permanent colonization of the New Netherlands was attempted, under the authority of the Dutch West India Company, the successor of the New Netherlands Company. They sent a company of thirty families of Walloons under the superintendence of Cornelius May, before spoken of, who arrived at the mouth of the Hudson in May, 1623. Some of them were located on Manhattan Island, to take possession there on behalf of the West India Company. Several families were sent for a like service to Long Island, and the balance to Fort Orange.

Manhattan Island, from its location, soon became the chief shipping port, and on the opposite or west bank of the river a small redoubt was thrown up, the immediate object in view being to secure the safe prosecution of traffic with the native tribes. This is the first positive evidence of any attempt at settlement in what is now Hudson County, although there is a belief that there was some kind of a trading post here contemporary with, or about the time of, the Dutch settlement in New York, in 1613. Whether it became permanent, or was only resorted to from time to time for the purpose of bartering with the Indians, is not positively known, although O'Callaghan's "Documentary History of New York" alludes to a settlement about this time. In a few years the trade with the natives was greatly extended, covering the whole country, even to the lakes.

On February 12, 1620, application was made on behalf of the "Brownists" for permission to found a colony in the New Netherlands. These were the Puritans who were driven from England by religious persecution during the reign of Elizabeth, and who reached Amsterdam in 1608. The next year they went to Leyden, and remained there eleven years. Having flourished and increased in numbers, they desired to teach the faith of the Cross to the savages, and to colonize a new empire on the shores of the Hudson under the auspices and protection of the Prince of Orange.

The statesmen of Holland were more ambitious in their designs, and rejected the petition of the Brownists, preferring that a great and powerful monopoly should grow up, whose concentrated wealth and energy should not only assist in the colonization of the New World, but be a powerful ally in any controversy with outside nations. The Brownists thereupon directed their course to the New England shores instead of the New Netherlands, landing at Plymouth Rock, December 21, 1620. The "Pilgrims," by this refusal, became the founders of New England, instead of, as was their intention, imparting their sturdy qualities to the territory about the Hudson.

May was made the first Director of the infant

colony, and his administration continued throughout the year 1624. The advantages of the country being now favorably known, other vessels with settlers arrived; and in 1625 the colony had increased to two hundred souls. May was succeeded by William Van Hulst as second Director. His administration, likewise, lasted only one year, and at the expiration of his time he returned to Holland. The West India Company now despatched Peter Minuit, of Wesel, to assume the chief command, as their third Director.

Up to 1626 the Dutch held their possessions only by right of occupation and discovery, but after many controversies with the Indians, the rights of the original owners were recognized, and they determined to purchase the territory from them. Shortly after Minuit's arrival, he opened negotiations with the savages, and concluded a treaty which conveyed the whole Island of Manhattan, about 22,000 acres of land, to the Dutch for the sum of sixty guilders, about $24 in our money. A fort was staked out at the southern end of the island, and houses were built, among them a stone building with thatched roof, for the Company's counting-house.

The States General, recognizing the great danger arising from controversies among the different bodies of settlers, determined early upon a fixed and uniform government, and consequently in 1629 established articles of order and government, that should be generally recognized in the different settlements. They authorized the various departments of the West India Company to appoint a Council of nine persons, who should have general authority and command over all the settlements in the New Netherlands. Local governments were formed under the *Schout* and *Schepens*, and *Krankbesoechers*, or "Comforters of the Sick," who on Sundays read to the people portions of the Scriptures, and the Creed.

Chapter VI.

DIFFICULTIES ENCOUNTERED.

It is interesting to note, as illustrative of the characteristics of the early Dutch settlers, an extract from a letter of George Bradford, Governor of New Plymouth. He says: "About Midmarch we received message from the Governor of the Dutch plantation, dated from the Manhattas, in the Fort Amsterdam, March 9, 1627. They" (the Dutch) "had traded in these northern parts, divers years after our coming. In their letter, they congratulate us on our prosperous, and praiseworthy undertaking, and government of our colony, with the presentation of their good will, and service to us, in all friendly kindness and good neighborhood ; offer us any of their goods, that may be serviceable to us, declare they shall take themselves, bound to accommodate, and help us with them for any wares we are pleased to deal for."

In response, Governor Bradford sent a letter of appreciation of the kindly offers, and signified his graceful acceptance; "alluding likewise to the hospitable asylum, afforded to the Pilgrims in Holland, when compelled to fly from the intolerant bigotry of their native land." The harmonious relations of the two colonies, thus amicably established, continued for many years, to their mutual advantage.

Notwithstanding these seemingly amicable relations, the fact remains that the growing prosperity of the Dutch excited a fear in the minds of their English neighbors lest their shrewd business tact and enterprise should overshadow them, and in time the Dutch become the recognized masters of the New World. As will be seen afterward, this led to the forcible attempt of the English government to displace and drive out the intruders, as they were considered from the English standpoint.

The previous occupation by the English of Virginia, and their successful development of its territory, in connection with their efforts from time to time to effect settlements within the jurisdiction of the New Netherlands, led the States General to make overtures to the British government to join with them and unite the trade of the two countries. These were rejected for the reason, as stated by an English statesman, "that in case of joining, if it be upon equal terms, the art and industry of their people, will wear out ours," a commentary upon the esteem in which the early Dutch settlers were held even at this date.

Previous to 1629, the Company did not secure much profit, on account of the heavy expenditures incurred in establishing and maintaining the settlements. In order, therefore, to incite private enterprise, and effect the more rapid development of the country, they offered special privileges to such of their own number as should within four years plant a colony of fifty adults in any part of New Netherlands, other than Manhattan Island. They should be recognized and acknowledged as Patroons, and have full control of and right to the territory assigned to them. This offer occasioned considerable strife and competition among the members of the Company, and the game of "freeze out" was played with as much shrewdness and vigor as at the present day. Some of the members thus secured possession of the choicest sections of land, to the detriment and loss of their less fortunate fellows. According to the complaints made, "some of the Directors helped themselves by the cunning tricks of the merchants, and made most advantageous selections, to the exclusion of others." This caused much dissatisfaction and jealousy, and led to fierce and open discussion. Through the pressure of public opinion, the fortunate Directors were compelled to relinquish their ill-gotten holdings, and re-convey their selections to the Company.

Chapter VII.

SETTLEMENT OF OLD BERGEN.

AMONG those who secured allotments under these privileges was Michael Pauw, Burgomaster of Amsterdam, and Lord of Achtienhoven, near Utrecht. By patent dated November 22, 1630, he obtained, with other lands, the plots "Aharsimus and Arresick, extending along the River Mauritius" (one of the early names of the Hudson), "and Island Manhatta on the east side, and the Island Hoboken Hacking on the north, and surrounded by marshes serving sufficiently for distinct boundaries." Pauw thus became invested with the title to the greater part of the territory now known as Hudson County, which was called Pavonia after him. Pauw never complied with the conditions of his grant, yet he assumed ownership, and held on to the property with grim determination. He must have energetically and successfully developed his holdings, for but two years later, in 1632, when Minuit was recalled, we find in the Reports, "that the Boueries and Plantations on the west side of the River, were in a prosperous condition."

Jan Evertsen Bout, who arrived June 17, 1634, became superintendent for Pauw, and settled at Communipau. He continued as his representative, bartering and trafficking with the Indians, etc., until he was succeeded by Cornelis Van Vorst, in 1636, who took up his residence at Aharsimus. He became of considerable importance during the early history of the colony. In 1641 he was one of the twelve selected to consult and advise with the Governor and Council, to effect a settlement of the

VAN VORST'S BOUERIE.

Indian difficulties; and he was one of the "Eight men" in 1643, and one of the "Nine men" in 1647 and 1650.

It is related that on one occasion Dominie Bogardus, Governor Van Twiller and Captain De Vries came to Pavonia, and were entertained by Van Vorst with old-fashioned Dutch hospitality. After indulging freely in the good things offered by their host, they took leave of him, full of enthusiasm by reason of their generous entertainment. As they embarked, Van Vorst, wishing to show his appreciation of their kindly feeling, ordered a parting salute to be fired. The wadding of the gun, falling on the thatched roof of his house, set it on fire, and notwithstanding his vigorous efforts, it was burned to the ground.

Complaints against Pauw, as one of the original officers of the Company who had taken advantage of his position, to secure the most valuable of the Company's holdings, continued to be brought forward. He was charged with having usurped the rights of others, and claiming ownership of his property without a shadow of right, for he had never complied with the requirements of the Company's grant. Pauw, however, positively refused to surrender his holdings. He seems to have been proof against all criticism and attack, and held on to his claim with Dutch tenacity. Finally, the feeling against him became so intense that on December 17, the Assembly of the Nine (the governing power) called him to account, and after much bargaining purchased his colony for 26,000 florins, or about $10,000.

Chapter VIII.

SETTLEMENT OF OLD BERGEN CONTINUED.

ON the recall of Minuit, in 1632, Wouter Van Twiller was appointed Director General, and arrived at New Amsterdam in the spring of 1633. His administration seems to have been singularly unfortunate; he was wanting in executive ability, being unable to control or direct others. He was finally removed, and was succeeded by William Kieft, in 1637.

Kieft was a politician of the more advanced type, whose peculiar talents would have received instant recognition in this present century. He was very energetic, with unbounded confidence in his own opinion and judgment, and but little respect for the advice of others. On his arrival he found matters in an unsatisfactory state, a general demoralization prevailing. He at once organized a Council, of which he retained entire control, and granted many favors, in the shape of offices and lands, by this means surrounding himself with obsequious and unscrupulous advisers, who were not only willing but eager, to support and advocate any measures that were pleasing to him. He was thus enabled to govern the colonies in an arbitrary manner, and ruled all with an iron hand. Being authorized to make all necessary expenditures and improvements at the fur-trading centers, he built extensive works at Manhatta, and ordered two houses to be built at Pavonia. One was built at Aharsimus (near Henderson and 5th streets), and occupied by Cornelis Van Vorst, and the other at Communipau by Jan Evertsen Bout.

The property occupied by Bout, when he was superintendent of Pauw, was, on the acquisition of the same by the Company, leased to him for six years from June 20, 1638, " at a yearly rent of one-fourth of the crops, whether of corn or produce, and every year two tuns of strong Beer, and twelve Capons free of expense." The property was described as follows: "A piece of land lying on the North River westward from Fort Amsterdam, before there pastured, and tilled by Jan Evertsen, named Gamoenapoeu, and Jan de Lacher's Hoeck " (so named from the occupant who was called John the Laugher, because of his mirth-loving propensities), " with the meadows as the same lay without the post and rail fence, containing 84 morgens." This is the property known as Communipaw, signifying Pauw's community, or settlement, comprising the territory south of the Mill Creek Point. Bout leased the land near Mill Creek Point to Egbert Wouterson, who resided there with his family.

Kieft's first conveyance of land in what is now Hudson County, was to Abraham Isaacsen Verplanck, dated May 1, 1638, of a tract at Paulus Hoeck, situated westward of the Island of Manhatta, and eastward of Aharsimus, extending from the North River into the valley, which runs around it there. The plot of ground now known as Hoboken was leased by Kieft to Aert Teunisen Van Putten, for twelve years from January 1, 1641, at a rental of the "fourth sheaf with which God Almighty shall favor the field." He formed here a bouerie, and erected a brew house. Thus was established an industry that has been successfully prosecuted at this place down to the present time.

Although Van Putten was killed by Indians in 1643, and his bouerie destroyed, the brew house remained standing. February 5, 1663, this property was granted by Gov. Stuyvesant to Nicholas Verlett, who settled before 1656 on a tract called Hobuck. His title was confirmed by Gov. Carteret by a new grant, May 12, 1668.

In 1641, Myndert Meyndertson was Patroon over a colony from Newark Bay to Tappan. With the exception of a bouerie west of Cavan Point, occupied by Dirck Straatmaker, these seem to have been the only settlements in what was the territory of Bergen, in 1643. What is now known as Jersey City Heights was covered with dense forests and frequented by native tribes and wild beasts, with possibly one or two clearings used for the cultivation of maize by the Indians; while in place of the crowded tenements and teeming industries of lower Jersey City, there were three islands or mounds, surrounded by lagoons and marshes, which at high tide, were covered with the water of the bay. One of these mounds was located in the territory south of York Street and east of Warren, and contained the trading post and fort of early days, already alluded to, and was afterward, in the Revolutionary times, the site of the battle of Paulus Hook. Another was located west of Barrow Street and between York Street and Railroad Avenue, extending to about the present line of Monmouth Street; while the third was the site in early days of Van Vorst's bouerie, where Dominie Bogardus and his friends were entertained, extending from about the present 6th Street to above Hamilton Square, and east of Cole Street to about Henderson.

Paulus Hook (*hook* meaning point) was the name by which in early days the southeasternmost section of Jersey City was known. Its name was due to the fact that one Michael Paulaz was stationed there by the West India Company to protect its interests.

De Vries states in his account of his voyages that, as he was about to return to Amsterdam (May, 1633), "coming to the boat on Long Island, night came on and the tide began to turn, so that we rowed to Pavonia; we were there well received by Michael Paulaz, an officer in the service of the Company."

Chapter IX.

THE NATIVE INHABITANTS.

THE native tribes found here by the early settlers were originally of very simple habits, but dominated greatly by their animal instincts. They were faithful to their friends, but vindictive and treacherous to any whom they regarded as enemies, and quick to resent any real or fancied injustice. They were a roving people, and their chief support came from hunting and fishing. They quickly perceived the advantage of trading with the whites, and had their treatment been more in accord with the requirements of civilization, much of the subsequent bloodshed might have been avoided. Free as the air they breathed, and accustomed to look upon the forests and rivers as means of furnishing themselves with food and traffic, they felt an ownership in them that would not brook outside interference. So when they saw the intruders gradually absorbing their territory and restricting their accustomed freedom, they felt a natural resentment, which was increased, not only by the unreasonableness of Governor Kieft's demands, but also by their unjust treatment in the matter of traffic. It is said that in bargaining with the Indians, a Dutchman's hand weighed one pound and his foot two, so that in some mysterious way it was made to appear that, no matter what the size of the Indian's bundle of peltry, its weight never exceeded the latter figure.

In the main, the desire of the early settlers seems to have been to treat the Indians with fairness and consideration, recompensing them for their property, and treating with them on an honorable footing. But unfortunately, as is always the case when new enterprises of the kind are attempted, unscrupulous men and adventurers were among the number, who, actuated and controlled simply by the desire of gain, disregarded the rights of the Indians, and by their unjust dealing awakened within them all their savage instincts. The unscrupulous treatment of them by Governor Kieft was for the greater part, if not entirely, the cause of the general outbreaks. Individual instances of injustice no doubt there were, that deserved summary treatment; but that whole tribes should unite in a war of extermination, was doubtless directly traceable to his unjust demands and double dealing.

Thus Kieft, by his injudicious treatment of the Indians, soon incurred their hostility. Although their savage nature and close proximity should have suggested constant watchfulness on the part of the settlers, Kieft, blinded by an undue sense of his own importance, treated them as if in fact they were his own subjects. He demanded of them a tribute of maize, furs and wampum, and when they demurred, threatened to employ all the force at his command to enforce his demands. This harsh treatment exasperated them, and henceforth the whole region was the scene of frequent outbreaks and difficulties. We find in the "Breeden Raet," printed in 1649, at Antwerp, as a result of the investigation instituted on account of the complaints against Kieft, the following: "They" (the natives) "asked why they should supply us with maize for nothing, since they paid as much as we asked, for everything they came to purchase of us. If, they said, we have ceded to you the country you are living in, we yet remain masters of what we have retained for ourselves. Have we not supplied you, Swannakens (or Dutchmen), on your first arrival here, and when you had no Mochols (or ships), with provisions for two whole winters? And had we not, you would have died of hunger. The delegates from all the savage tribes, such as the Raritans, the Hacquinnas, the Tappanders, and others had got as many objections to make as there were points to discuss.

"They however separated peaceably, contenting themselves with giving us no contributions, nor asking any from us. Director Kieft, seeing himself deprived of this contribution, which he was very greedy of by so many reasons, and also because it would disgrace him in the eyes of his countrymen, invented other means to satisfy his insatiable, avaricious soul."

The Indians positively refused to supply "maize for nothing," and showed their resentment by harassing the settlers in every possible way. Their hostility assumed an active form, and as opportunity offered, they carried off and killed the cattle found wandering through the woods. They secured fire-arms from some of the unscrupulous traders, who, incited by greed of gain, disregarded the positive commands of the West India Company, not to barter fire-arms, and "traded enough guns, bullets, and fire-arms, to furnish four hundred warriors." The Indians soon became proficient in the use of these, and consequently more to be dreaded.

Chapter X.

DISSATISFACTION WITH KIEFT AND CAUSES THEREFOR.

THE people were anxious to maintain peace with the savages, and were indignant with Kieft for his harshness. He thereupon called them together for consultation, and chose twelve select men to consult and advise with the Director and Council. They counselled moderation, and were to be notified by the Governor before any action should be taken. Notwithstanding this, Kieft became more decided and exacting in his demands, and determined to enforce them at any cost. As a preparation, he ordered the residents of Manhatta and the vicinity to arm themselves, and at the firing of three guns to repair to the place appointed for service.

Shortly after this, some of the Company's men landed on Staten Island, which had been settled by De Vries, and stole some hogs belonging to him. For this theft, the Raritan Indians were blamed, and Governor Kieft sent a party of fifty soldiers and twenty sailors to attack them and destroy their corn, unless they should make reparation. This was refused, several of the Indians were killed, and their crops were destroyed. In retaliation, the Indians attacked De Vries' plantation on Staten Island; whereupon Kieft issued a proclamation offering ten fathoms of wampum for every head of that tribe, and twenty fathoms for heads of actual murderers. This offer excited the cupidity of the other tribes, and intensified the strife among them. To obtain this reward, much innocent blood was shed and ill feeling engendered.

The Indians were divided into different tribes and languages, each tribe living separate and apart by itself, and having a chief to whom it was subject. These tribes differed greatly in characteristics, some of them being naturally of a friendly disposition, while others were quite the reverse. These differences often led to feuds and strife among them, and there was a natural enmity between the Indians inhabiting the upper Hudson (the Iroquois and Mohawks), who were by nature fierce and warlike, and those who were located about the mouth of the Hudson, (the Delawares), who were more pacific in their nature.

In 1643, one of these periodical outbreaks occurred, and the fierce Mohawks made an attack upon the lower tribes, on the west side of the river. Many of these were slain and made prisoners, and many fled to Manhatta, and afterwards to Pavonia, where they encamped on the 22nd of February, 1643, at Jan de Lacher Hoeck, behind the settlement of Egbert Wouterson, and near Jan Evertsen Bout's bouerie (near the intersection of Pine Street with New Jersey Central R. R.) Kieft thought this afforded him a favorable opportunity to punish the Indians for their rebellion, and at the same time enforce his demands to their fullest extent.

"OLD BERGEN."

He thereupon issued the following order: "Sergeant Rudolf is commanded and authorized to take under his command a troop of soldiers, and lead them to Pavonia, and drive away and destroy the savages lying behind Jan Evertsen Bout, to spare as is possible their wives and children. The exploit should be executed at night, with the greatest caution and prudence."

MILL CREEK.

In pursuance of this order, the sergeant and eighty soldiers embarked in boats, crossed to the shores of Pavonia, and, rounding the southerly point of Paulus Hook, pulled for the high bank at the mouth of the

Mill Creek (near Jersey Avenue and Phillip Street). Cautiously climbing over this bank, they came suddenly on the unsuspecting Indians, and slaughtered many of them, sparing neither the old, the women nor the children. So thoroughly were the survivors deceived as to the origin of this attack, that they fled for protection to the Dutch at Fort Amsterdam, believing that they had been surprised and attacked by the Mohawks. They were, however, soon undeceived, and then commenced a relentless war.

All the tribes between the Raritan and the Connecticut now buried their individual resentments, and combined in a war for the extermination of the whites; and all those not in the immediate vicinity of Fort Amsterdam, were in constant danger from the tomahawk and scalping-knife. So general was the uprising, and so energetic and relentless was the attack of the Indians, that in a short time the whole country was wrested from the whites, and the savages again roamed unmolested over the soil.

Peace was finally concluded, but being on unsatisfactory terms to the Indians, it was not of long duration. They could not so readily forget the wrongs they had suffered, and felt that they were unavenged. They therefore broke out into open hostility again, determined to obtain full and complete satisfaction. Kieft, now thoroughly alarmed, sought the assistance of the people, whom he had hitherto slighted. Eight men were selected, instead of twelve, for conference with the Council.

Self-preservation compelled them to active measures,

and war was determined upon; the people were armed, and so stationed as to protect the outlying settlements. But the savages, by means of their peculiar, stealthy manner of warfare, were enabled to greatly harass the settlers, and we find the four boueries in Pavonia laid waste—Bout's, Wouterson's, Stofflesen's and Teunisen's. Every bouerie and plantation was destroyed, and the cattle killed or driven away.

These troubles produced much discontent among the colonists, and, recognizing that their great misfortunes had been brought upon them by the inordinate ambition and misgovernment of Kieft, the people were aroused, and sent protests to the home government, again demanding his removal.

Chapter XI.

CONTINUANCE OF INDIAN TROUBLES.

KIEFT was superseded July 28, 1646, by Peter Stuyvesant, who arrived at Fort Amsterdam May 11, 1647. He found the situation somewhat alarming, for crime was rampant, and anarchy prevailed. By the exercise of his administrative ability, he succeeded in restoring confidence among the colonists. The Indians, however, claiming that the conditions of the treaty of peace were not complied with, again became dissatisfied and aggressive. In order to effect a satisfactory arrangement and avoid the disasters of another war, nine men were selected by the Directors to advise the government when requested. Michael Jansen of Pavonia, and Cornelis Van Vorst, were of this number. Through the exercise of diplomacy, and a conciliatory policy, the settlers had no special difficulty with the Indians for some years, and until 1655 they gave their full attention to the improvement and development of their holdings.

The West India Company having relinquished its monopoly of the Indian trade on payment of a small duty by individual traders, the enterprise of the latter made itself felt. The colonists spread themselves throughout the country, and many came from the

Fatherland to engage in what now promised to be a profitable occupation. Each sought to advance his own interest, and many lived among the Indians in order to trade advantageously with them.

Houses were hastily constructed of stone or logs, as either material was the more easily obtainable when a settlement was made. They were usually covered with branches, thatched over with reeds or grass collected from the surrounding marshes, and large stone fireplaces were built, connected with an outside chimney or flue made of scantling or the bark of trees.

Being thus conveniently located, the settlers were enabled the more easily to gather in from their savage neighbors large quantities of skins and furs, for which a ready market was found at the Company's trading post on Manhattan Island. Soon, however, competition became so fierce that deception and underhand practices were indulged in, and this unjust treatment again excited the natural jealousy and distrust of the savages. Notwithstanding their protests, the greed for gain blinded the settlers as to their danger, and their unjust exactions and oppressions continued.

The Indians, recognizing the advantage of the market brought to their doors by the adventurous whites, sullenly submitted to the injustice of their treatment, rather than, by the exercise of their superior force, destroy such market by the extermination of their oppressors. However, frequent outbreaks occurred, and a feeling of unrest and insecurity was excited. Constant watchfulness on the part of the settlers was required to prevent surprise by the Indians, who were ready, on the slightest pretext and at the first favorable opportunity, to avenge their wrongs. The houses of the whites became their fortresses, and the common danger allayed to a great extent the bitter feeling among them engendered by their rivalry in trade.

In spite of the unsettled state of affairs during this interval, numerous grants of land had been made in Pavonia. Maryn Adriaensen, who was one of the Twelve, secured a grant of fifty morgens at Weehawken ; Dirck Zieken, a plantation below Communipau, back of Cavan Point ; Jacob Jacobson Roy, one at Constable Hook ; Claas Carstensen, land at Greenville ; and others between Communipau and Bergen Point.

During the absence of Gov. Stuyvesant, who, having determined to expel the Swedes settled at and about South River, was directing in person an expedition against them, new difficulties arose. The Dutch burghers at Manhatta had experienced great annoyance from frequent depredations upon their fruit and vegetables by unknown parties. Their gardens were unusually exposed, as they were located in the rear of their dwellings and extended down to the water's edge, thus affording free access to marauders, who could stealthily approach by boat from the opposite shore, and readily escape in case of interruption. The burghers determined upon stringent measures, and strict watch was kept. One night in July, 1654, the watchman, discovering that some one was stealing peaches, fired his blunderbuss with such effect that an Indian maid was killed, while the rest of the party took to their boats and escaped. This seemed the

"OLD BERGEN." 45

one thing necessary to excite the already inflamed savages to commence their work of devastation.

On the 15th of September, a force of five hundred warriors in sixty-four canoes, secretly landed at Manhatta and attempted to secure the murderer. They scattered through the streets, but were discovered by the guard, who attacked them and drove them to their canoes. Crossing the river to Pavonia, the savages destroyed the houses there, laid waste the plantations, destroyed a large amount of maize, killed or carried off a number of cattle, and took with them some of the settlers whom they had captured. Pavonia was again desolated, and the survivors fled for safety to New Amsterdam, so that once more the savages held unrestricted sway over the territory. Emboldened by their successes, the latter hovered around the outskirts of New Amsterdam, with the determination of now securing a full recompense for the indignities heaped upon them in the past by the injudicious whites.

The close watch of the force protecting the town foiled their efforts, and the action taken by Governor Stuyvesant, who hastened his return upon hearing of this attack, prevented any further efforts. He immediately adopted measures for the full protection of the province. He endeavored to conciliate the Indians, and entered into negotiations with them for the ransoming of their prisoners. Pending the result, a large body of savages with their prisoners were stationed at Paulus Hook. Their proximity, and evident reluctance to hasten negotiations, produced considerable excitement at New Amsterdam. The relatives and friends of those who had been captured were naturally indignant at the delay, and they made threats against the Indians and attempted retaliatory measures. To lessen the danger of an outbreak, the authorities ordered that no intercourse of any kind should be had with the savages, and continued their efforts to secure a peaceful termination to their negotiations. After considerable bartering, a price was agreed upon, which being paid, the captives were released, and the second general Indian war ended.

Michael Jansen, who was living with his family at Communipau, escaped the general slaughter; but in view of the unsettled condition of affairs, he had removed to New Amsterdam, so that there was not left at this time a single white man within the limits of this territory.

Chapter XII.

PRECAUTIONARY MEASURES ADOPTED.

In a short time, however, a few of the colonists returned to their ruined homes and endeavored to restore them to their former condition. The difficulty of protecting isolated or scattered settlements being recognized, the Director General and Council passed an ordinance January 18, 1656, setting forth as follows: "In consequence of the separate dwellings of the country people, many murders of people, killing and destruction of cattle, and burning of houses, have been committed and perpetrated by the Indians, the most of which might have been, with God's help, prevented and avoided, if the good inhabitants of this province had settled themselves together in the form of towns, villages and hamlets, like our neighbors of New England, who, because of their combination and compact residences, have never been subject to such—at least not to so many and such general disasters, which have been caused, next to God's righteous chastisement, on account of our sins by tempting the savage barbarians thereto by the separate residences of the country people.

"The Director General and Council, aforesaid, do hereby not only warn their good subjects, but likewise charge and command them, to concentrate them-

selves by next spring in the form of towns, villages
and hamlets, so that they may be the more effectually
protected, maintained and defended, against all assaults and attacks of the barbarians, by each other,
and by the military entrusted to the Director General
and Council. Furthermore, in order to prevent a too
sudden conflagration, they do ordain, that from now
henceforth, no houses shall be covered with straw or
reed, nor any more chimneys be constructed of clap-
boards or wood."

The next year the ordinance was reaffirmed, and
the people commanded to respect its provisions. The
horrors of Indian warfare were so great, and the feeling of insecurity so general, that the settlers with few
exceptions delayed returning to Pavonia, and the
country remained almost desolate. In order to remove any cause for friction with the Indians on
account of adverse claims to their territory, and to
reassure the timid settlers, Governor Stuyvesant and
the Council of New Netherlands purchased of the Indians, January 30, 1658, a tract of land by the following description :

" Lying on the west bank of the Hudson, beginning at
the Great Clip " (meaning Rock), " above Weehawken,
and from thence right through the lands till above the
island of Siskakes " (Secaucus), " and thereupon thence
to the Kill von Kull, and so along to the Constable
Hook, and from the Constable Hook again to the
aforesaid Clip at Weehawken, with all the lands,
islands, channels, and valleys therein comprehended—
for eighty fathom of wampum, twenty fathom of

cloth, twelve brass kettles, and one-half barrel strong beer."

This was done at Fort Amsterdam and signed with the marks of the Indians, after the cargoes were delivered to their hands, the 30th day of January, Anno Domini, 1658. The following are their names:

THERINCQUES,   WAWAPEHACK,
SAGHKOW,   BOMOKAN,
SAMES,   WEWENATOKEE,
KOGHKENNINGH,   MEMIWOKAN,
WAIRIMUS CONWEE,

Witness: SAMES, otherwise called JOB.

By this deed the Indians relinquished all their right and title in and to the territory lying between the Hudson River, and the Hackensack and Newark Bay (comprising the old Township of Bergen). This same territory was assessed in 1901 on a valuation of about $150,000,000. This purchase by the Council tended to allay to a great extent the hostility of the Indians, and the settlers who had been driven away were anxious to return to their former fields. They were enabled to develop their holdings without much interference, but so great was the expense they were subjected to, on account of the general destruction of their buildings, that they petitioned the Council to exempt them from the payment of tithes or taxes for a few years. This petition was signed by Michael Jansen Vreeland, Claas Jansen Bacher, Claas Petersen Garrabrant Cos, Jans Captain, Dirck Sekier, Dirck Claersen and Lysbet Tysen. Whereupon the Council made an order as follows, dated January 22nd, 1658:

"The suppliants are permitted, in consideration of the reasons explained in their petition, the privilege of exemption from the payment of tithes, and the burthens attached to these, during six years, provided that they, in conformity to the order and placards of the Director General and Council, concentrate themselves in the form of a village, at least of ten or twelve families together; to become in future more secure, and easier to receive aid for defence, in similar disastrous occurrences."

On this encouragement, the settlers began to reoccupy their plantations and boueries, but seem to have been averse to collecting together in villages, as conditioned. The following order was thereupon issued: "In order to prevent, and in future put a stop, as much as possible, to such massacres, murders and burning by cruel barbarians at the separate dwellings, the Director General and Council of New Netherlands do therefore notify and order all isolated farmers in general, and each in particular, wherever they may reside, without any distinction of person, to remove their houses, goods and cattle, before the last of March, or at latest the middle of April, and convey them to the village nearest and most convenient to them; or with the previous knowledge and approval of the Director General and Council, to a favorably situated and defensible spot, in a new Palisade village, to be hereafter formed, when all those who apply shall be shown and granted suitable lots by the Director General and Council, or their agents; so that the Director General and Council, in case of any difficulty with the cruel barbarians, would be better able to assist, maintain and protect their good subjects, with the force entrusted to them by God, and the Supreme Authority—on pain of confiscation of all such goods as shall be found after the aforesaid time, in separate dwellings and farm-houses."

Chapter XIII.

BERGEN.

As a result of this order, several petitions were submitted " to settle on the maize land behind Communipau," and on the 16th of August, 1660, "several inhabitants of this province " petitioned for the right to cultivate farms and plantations on the west side of the river, behind Communipau, and to make there a village, or concentration. This was granted, " provided that such village shall be founded and placed on a convenient spot that may be defended with ease, and to be selected by the Director General, and Council, or Commissioners." This grant was, however, on condition that all who applied should share with others by lot, should send at least one person capable of bearing arms, for general service, and should make a beginning to erect buildings six weeks after the drawing of lots.

It must have been shortly after the granting of the petition above mentioned, that the village of Bergen was founded, as in a deed dated the following November, the location of the land conveyed is described as " near the village of Bergen, in the new maize land." This belief is strengthened by the following statement, made some time in 1664, which sets forth that the whole territory was given or granted to the inhabitants of Bergen in 1661, thus proving beyond doubt that the organization of the village had been accomplished before this date:

"We, underwritten, the late Director General and Council of New Netherlands, hereby certify and declare that in the year one thousand six hundred and sixty-one, by us underwritten, in quality as aforesaid, was given and granted to the inhabitants of the Village of Bergen, the lands with the meadows thereunto annexed, situated on the west side of the North River, in Pavonia, in the same manner, as the same was by us underwritten, purchased of the Indians, and as the same was to us delivered by the said Indians, pursuant to an instrument of sale, and delivery thereof, being under date of the 3rd of January, A. D. 1658, with this express condition, and promise, that the aforesaid inhabitants of the before named village, shall not be prejudiced in their outdrift, by means of any private collective dwellings (saving only the right of the then already cultivated farms at Gemoenepau), but that all such, who have any lands, within the district of the before named village, and especially at Pemrepogh and Mingackgue, all such owners shall be obliged to remove their dwellings, and place them in the village or town of Bergen, or by or about the neighborhood of Gemoenepau before named. Conditioned, however, that the aforesaid owners (in case they should desire the same) should be permitted to share, and divide with the inhabitants, of the before named village, or town, in the common lands of the said town, and in the place, and stead of their lands, lying at

Pemrepogh and Mingackgue before named (and especially that the meadows lying near the village or town of Bergen, where the same begins, at the west side along the Kill von Kull should be, and belong to, and for the use of, the before named inhabitants of Bergen).

"And further, we the underwritten, certify and declare, that Michael Jansen, deceased (before or about the time that the aforesaid village or town was laid out), for himself as also for, and in behalf of, his brother-in-law, Nicholas Jansen Barker, did, in our presence, renounce all the right they had to the pasture ground, laying behind Gemoenepau, for a common outdrift and pasture between the aforesaid village or town, and the neighborhood of Gemoenepau before named.

"And lastly, that no more lands were given or granted to Dirck Clausen than Rightpocques, with the meadows thereunto belonging, as by the ground brief thereof may further appear.

"In testimony of the truth we have signed these with our own hands in New York, the 26th October, A. D., 1661."

Signed: P. STUYVESANT.
NICASIUS DE SILLE.

Many and varied suggestions have been made as to the origin and cause of the name of Bergen. Some claim it to have been so called after the capital of Norway, others derive the name from a small town in Holland, others think that the name denoted a place of safety, and others assert that the village was named on account of its location. And what is more plausible than this latter explanation? As the sturdy Hollander, accustomed to the marsh and low land of his native country, saw the hill rising up out of the surrounding marsh, and stretching in unbroken front far to the north, what is more natural than that he should exclaim in wonder, " Berg! Bergen!" (The hill! The place of the hill!)

The commanding position of the territory, making it capable of easy defence and protection, together with its proximity to New Amsterdam, doubtless determined the selection of this locality. The town was directed to be laid out by Jacques Cortelyou, the first surveyor of New Amsterdam. It was in the form of a square, eight hundred feet long on each side, with two cross streets meeting at right angles in the center, where a vacant space was reserved, one hundred and sixty feet by two hundred and twenty-five feet. These streets divided the plot into four quarters, which were subdivided into building lots. Along the outer side of the plot palisades were erected, with gates at the termination of the cross streets, which were closed at night, or when any attack of Indians was threatened. The original plan is still preserved at Bergen Square, Academy Street and Bergen Avenue being the intersecting cross streets, while Tuers and Idaho Avenues on the east and west, and Newkirk and Vroom Streets on the north and south, mark the line of the palisades.

The houses of the settlers were erected within the enclosure, in accordance with the condition of the grant of the Council, for their better protection against Indian attacks; while their farms extended out into the adjoining country. These were called *buytentuyn,* or outside gardens. They were thoroughly cultivated, and in part used for grazing, and the cattle were driven within the palisades nightly, or when the

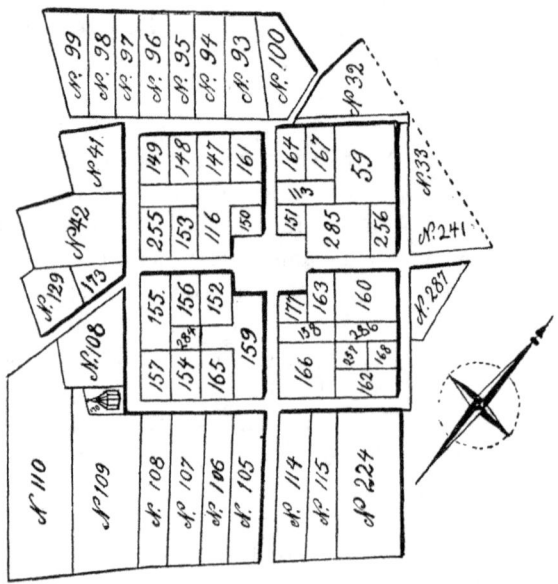

PLAN OF BERGEN.

savages became unusually active. On such occasions, water was obtained at great risk, and much suffering was caused. Whereupon the Schout and Schepens ordained, that a well for the public accommodation be constructed within the enclosure. This action was ratified by the Council at New Amsterdam, February

9, 1662, and a well was dug in the center of the square, a long sweep erected for raising the water, and troughs placed about it from which the cattle might drink. This well was used for a long time, but was finally filled up and covered over. During the war of 1812, a Liberty Pole was erected in it.

This pole was surmounted by a gilded star, which, flashing in the sunlight from its prominent position, was visible from a long distance. It became a landmark especially for wary fishermen to locate the favorite haunts of the finny tribe in the waters of New York and Newark Bays. Their custom was to run an imaginary line from it to some prominent object on the opposite shore, which was crossed at the spot sought for by a similar line at right angles. This pole was taken down in 1870, when the car tracks were laid. As the square still retains its original size and shape, the exact location of the old well can be approximated, as it was dug in its center.

A curious document dated April 1, 1661, sets forth the lease of a lot, conditioning the construction of a house thirty feet long, and barn fifty feet long, to be built along the palisades of the village. "The lessor to deliver in March, a plow and wagon for joint use; also on halves, two young cows, and two three-year-old oxen, on half risk; and the following spring, two more of each. The occupant to pay the first and second years, fifteen pounds of butter for each cow, and for the remaining four years of the term, two hundred guilders, in coin or good wampum."

Chapter XIV.

BERGEN CONTINUED.

As the population of the town and the surrounding country increased, it was felt that some more convenient manner of settling the disputes and difficulties that were continually arising, should be determined upon, than had previously existed. The Court of Burgomasters and the Schepens at New Amsterdam exercised jurisdiction on the west side of the river as well as in that place; and not being in possession of actual knowledge of existing conditions, they were unable to decide promptly or accurately the questions submitted to them. A petition was thereupon presented to the Governor and Council at New Amsterdam, asking for relief, and praying for the establishment of a "local court of justice," which should determine and adjudicate such questions as should arise, affecting the petitioners.

In response thereto, the following ordinance was passed September 5, 1661, by the Director and Council of New Netherlands, erecting a court of justice at Bergen: "That their Honors do not hope or wish for anything else than the prosperity and welfare of their good inhabitants in general, and in particular, of the people residing in the village of Bergen, situated on the west side of the North River; and considering the increase in population of said village, therefore resolved, to favor its inhabitants with an Inferior Court of Justice, and to constitute it, as much as possible, and as the circumstances of the country permit, according to the laudable custom of the City of Amsterdam, in Holland, but so that all judgments shall be subject to reversal by, and an appeal to, the Director General, and Council of New Netherlands, to be by their Honors finally disposed of.

"It is necessary to choose as judges, honest, intelligent persons, owners of real estate, who are lovers of peace, and well affected subjects of their lords and patrons and of their Supreme Government established here, promoters and professors of the Reformed Religion as it is at present taught, in conformity of the Word of God, and the order of the Synod of Dortrecht; which court for the present, until it shall be herein otherwise ordained by the said lords, patrons, or their deputy, shall consist of one Schout, who shall convoke the appointed Schepens, and preside at the meeting, and with three Schepens, to which office are for the present time, and ensuing year, commencing the 20th of this month, elected by the Director General and Council, Michael Jansen, Harman Smeeman, and Caspar Stynmets.

"The Schout and Schepens are authorized in case of any special emergency or necessity, to enact some Ordinances for the greater advantage and contentment of the aforesaid village; respecting surveys, highways, outlets, ports, and fences of lands; laying out of gardens, orchards, and such like matters . . . . Also in regard to the buildings of churches, schools, and similar public works, and the means by which same are to be effected. But to commit to writing their opinions thereupon, and the reasons therefor, and submit them to the Director General and Council, in order that they may be approved and confirmed."

These magistrates were obliged to take oath, among other things, that they would "maintain the Reformed Religion and no other, and support the same." The first Schout was Tilman Van Vleck, who was commissioned the same date, and the first municipal government and court in the State of New Jersey was thus constituted :

    Tilman Van Vleck, Schout.
    Michael Jansen,
    Harman Smeeman, } Schepens.
    Caspar Stynmets,

The erection of this court, elevating the little village into the dignity of a seat of justice and government for the surrounding territory, doubtless attached its name to all the neighboring dependencies, and although many of them retained locally the name by which each little settlement was originally known, yet from this time forth, they were all referred to and designated under the general name of Bergen. Thus, although it is historically recorded that New Jersey was first settled by the Dutch at a place called Bergen, it is well substantiated that to Pavonia, or more properly to Communipau, to be locally exact, must be accorded the honor of first receiving, within what is now the Province of New Jersey, the adventurous navigators who left the Fatherland in quest of the riches that were popularly supposed to lie hidden within the unexplored region of the New World. Communipau, from its location, was probably the most inviting spot on the western shores of the Hudson; being well wooded and

COMMUNIPAW IN EARLY DAYS.

possessing a natural, well sheltered harbor, with high ground connected directly with the adjacent hills, it commended itself to the thrifty settler as a desirable location for a home. Not only were the waters that laved its shores, stocked with shell-fish, but in their regular seasons, schools of sturgeon, mackerel and shad furnished means of remunerative employment to all, while in the interval the fruitful soil recompensed the laborer with an abundance of the products of the earth. Tradition says that the Indians early perceived its natural advantages, and after the settlement of the Indian difficulties, still clung to its shores, and joined with the Dutch settlers, living at peace with them for some time, fishing in the adjoining waters, and hunting in the woods that covered the neighboring heights.

But as the white men increased in numbers, the natives were gradually forced back along the shore, and finally were compelled to move westward to escape their encroachments; and yet in some cases there was such strong attachment to some of the old families, that there were individual instances of Indians who refused to move away with their tribe. Continuing their friendships, they retained their wigwams, and ended their days within sight of the water on which they had so often sailed with their birch canoes. As was said to an old settler by one of the last survivors of the tribe: "My parents and parents' parents were not savages, but good people, who feared the God with all the simplicity of their primitive natures. There was no blood on their hands, and no scalps at their belts; but good or bad, they had to go according to what the white man calls progress and civilization."

Washington Irving thus humorously describes the discovery and settlement of Communipau: "The Goede Vrouw came to anchor at the mouth of the Hudson, a little to the east of Gibbet Island.

"OLD BERGEN." 63

Here, lifting up their eyes, they beheld, on what is at present called the Jersey Shore, a small Indian village pleasantly embowered in a grove of spreading elms, and the natives all collected on the beach, gazing in stupid admiration at the Goede Vrouw. A boat was immediately despatched to enter into a treaty with them, and approaching the shore, hailed them through a trumpet, in the most friendly terms; but so horribly confounded were these poor savages at the tremendous and uncouth sound of the Low Dutch language, that they one and all took to their heels, and scampered over the Bergen hills, nor did they stop until they had buried themselves, head and ears, in the marshes on the other side, where they all miserably perished to a man, and their bones being collected, and decently covered by the Tammany Society of that day, formed that singular mound called Rattlesnake Hill, which rises out of the center of the salt marshes, a little to the east of the Newark Causeway. . . . Accordingly they descended from the Goede Vrouw, men, women and children in goodly groups, as did the animals of yore from the ark, and formed themselves into a thriving settlement, which they called by the Indian name Communipau."

Chapter XV.

BERGEN CONTINUED.

THE settlement at Communipau, being located within easy reach of New Amsterdam, flourished greatly, and it was determined to establish a village there. Jacques Cortelyou was ordered, on the 8th of September, 1661, to survey, and lay out into lots, the land about Communipau. The lots thus surveyed fronted on the Bay, and were about two hundred feet deep. It was decided to erect defences against the Indians, but their building was delayed on account of the unwillingness of some of the settlers to engage in the work, for the reason that they did not apprehend any immediate attack by the savages. Complaint was made to the Director General and Council, and they were asked to enforce the ordinance. The Council urged and commanded the construction of the defences, but no decided action was taken, and as a matter of fact, the fortifications were never completed.

The people at Bergen and the dependent villages, settled upon the lots, as selected, by virtue of the provisions of the charter, but had neglected to secure patents. This created much confusion and trouble, and on September 15, 1661, all the inhabitants were ordered within three months to have their claims surveyed and marked, and on exhibition of returns to secure regular patents. This was done, and all disputes and controversies ended for the time. The titles to lands became vested in the parties as adjudged.

With increasing population, better facilities for reaching Manhatta were demanded, and December 22, 1661, Wm. Jansen petitioned the Director and Council to ratify a permission given him by the Schout and Schepens of Bergen, to work a ferry between Bergen and the Island of Manhatta. This was granted, and in pursuance thereof, a ferry from Communipau was established. This was for many years the only authorized mode of communication with Manhatta. The ferryman was regularly licensed, and rates were established for daytime and fair weather; but by night or in stormy weather, they were to be as the parties might agree. The ferryman was to keep his boat in readiness at all times, but more particularly on three days of the week, to be agreed upon unanimously by the inhabitants of Bergen and Communipau. From this ferry at Communipau a road extended along the route of the present Communipaw Avenue, and thence through Summit Avenue, to and connecting with, Academy Street, one of the cross streets of the Town of Bergen before mentioned.

In 1662 we find the ferryman complaining that the freeholders of Bergen authorized the inhabitants to ferry themselves over, as they pleased, much to his loss and discomfort. His protest seems to have been of little avail, for until very recent years, the old settlers and their descendants continued the practice of transporting themselves and their belongings to and from the city of New York. It is related that on one occasion, when one of our good Dutch burghers with his family was returning from market, an immense fish in its gambols leaped from the water, and, accidentally landing in the boat, crashed through the bottom. Whereupon the goodwife, drawing about herself her voluminous petticoats, calmly seated herself in the hole, effectually stopping the inflow of water, and enabling all to reach shore in safety. A striking instance of her presence of mind and general adaptability.

The isolated position of the settlement of Bergen town, back from the river, and surrounded by dense woods, which were populated by crafty Indians, rendered the town liable to attack at any time. Wherefore, in order that it should at all times be sufficiently protected, an ordinance was passed November 15, 1663, to the following effect : "All those who claim any lots in the aforesaid village shall, within twenty-four hours after notice being served, furnish and maintain for each lot, one man able to bear arms; and in case of their neglect to comply, their property is in danger of confiscation." October 18, 1664, in the accounts rendered to the Council, we find an item of twelve pounds of powder fired from two cannon about eight o'clock in the evening as a warning to the people to be on their guard, "as two Christians on their way from Bergen to Communipau were this day murdered by the Indians."

Chapter XVI.

THE CURRENCY, AND CAPTURE BY ENGLAND.

Up to about this time the Dutch carried on the traffic with New Netherlands without much rivalry. Although isolated attempts at competition were made by some English merchants, they never achieved much success. Natural business jealousies, however, excited frequent controversies between the settlers of New England and those of New Netherlands, and continual disputes arose as to ownership and boundary of territory. The increasing prosperity of the Dutch province, likewise, soon revived the interest of the English in what they claimed to be their possessions, and the fear of rivalry in the commercial world prompted the New Englanders to apply to the home government for relief and assistance. Charles II. determined to secure this extensive and growing trade. Basing his claim on the discovery of the Cabots, fortified by the fact that Henry Hudson was an Englishman, he granted a patent to the Duke of York (his brother) in 1664, giving him the entire territory of New Netherlands, and the power to govern the same.

Bergen had at this time become a place of considerable importance, and the settlement gradually assumed a condition of prosperity, so much so, that in a letter written at the time of the granting of the patent to the

Duke of York, it is described as "well inhabited by a sober and industrious people, who have necessary provisions for themselves and families, and for the comfortable entertainment of travellers and strangers." They industriously cultivated the ground, and found an excellent market for their products in Manhatta. Their connection with this place was by row or sail boats, the latter called periaguas.

The currency in vogue at this time as a medium of exchange was made from shells, and called wampum or seawant. It was of two colors, black and white, the black being of double the value of the white; three black or six white equalled a stiver, and twenty stivers made a guilder, which was worth forty cents of United States money. But as its manufacture was practically free to all persons, everyone had his own mint, and the benefit (?) of free and unlimited coinage was fully enjoyed. It may be readily supposed that the shrewd business thrift of at least some of the early settlers, suggested opportunities for reaping great advantages. At least the actual effect produced may be estimated from the following proclamation issued in 1690:

"The Director General and Counsellors of New Netherlands, to all persons who may see these Presents or hear them read, send greeting:

"Whereas with great concern we have observed both now and for a long time past the depreciation and corruption of the loose seawant, etc., whereby occasion is given for repeated complaints from the inhabitants, that they cannot go with such seawant to the market, nor yet procure for themselves any commodity, not even a white loaf, we ordain that no loose seawant shall be a legal tender except the same be strung on one string ; that six white or three black shall pass for one stiver, and of base seawant, shall pass eight white and four black for one stiver."

Manuscript Record of the Province, dated 1659, states as follows: " The N. E. People make use of it " (wampum) " as a means of barter, not only to carry away the best cargoes which we send thither, but to accumulate a large quantity of beaver and other furs, by which the Company is defrauded of her revenues, and the merchants disappointed in making returns with that speed with which they might wish to meet their engagements, while their commissioners and the inhabitants remain overstocked with seawant, a sort of currency of no value except with the New Netherland savages."

Irving facetiously alludes to the effect produced as follows : " It " (seawant) " had an intrinsic value among the Indians, who used it to ornament their robes and moccasins, but among the honest burghers it had no more intrinsic value than those rags which form the paper currency of modern days. This consideration, however, had no weight with William Kieft. He began by paying all the servants of the Company, and all the debts of Government in strings of wampum. He sent emissaries to sweep the shores of Long Island, which was the Ophir of this modern Solomon, and abounded in shell fish. These were transported in loads to New Amsterdam, coined into Indian money, and launched into circulation.

"And now, for a time, affairs went swimmingly; money became as plentiful as in the modern days of paper currency, and to use the popular phrase, 'a wonderful impulse was given to public prosperity.' Yankee trade poured into the province, buying everything they could lay their hands on, and paying the worthy Dutchmen their own price—in Indian money. If the latter, however, attempted to pay the Yankees in the same coin for their tinware and wooden bowls, the case was altered; nothing could do but Dutch guilders, and such like metallic currency. What was more, the Yankees introduced an inferior kind of wampum, made of oyster shells, with which they deluged the province, carrying off in exchange all the silver and gold, Dutch herrings, and Dutch cheeses. Thus early did the knowing men of the East manifest their skill in bargaining the New Amsterdamers out of the oyster and leaving them the shell.

"William the Testy found out that his grand project of finance was turned against him by his Eastern neighbors, when he found that the Yankees had established a kind of mint at Oyster Bay, where they were coining up all the oyster banks."

On the 25th of May, 1664, a fleet was sent from England under Col. Richard Nicolls, to enforce the claim of the English government against the New Netherlands. This fleet arrived in July and demanded the surrender of New Amsterdam. The people of Bergen determined to strengthen and increase the defences of the town. On the 21st of February, commissioners were appointed to erect block houses for its protection.

Whether they were ever completed, and where they were located, is not positively known, although tradition asserts that there was one erected at the southeast corner of the palisades (corner of Tuers Avenue and Vroom Street) when the village was founded, and if so, this was probably strengthened at this time. There was likewise a fort or redoubt thrown up at the brow of the hill, near Academy and Front Streets. The Dutch, however, surrendered in the face of the superior force of the English, having received favorable conditions; and on the 3rd of September, 1664, the government of the colony passed into the hands of the English. Col. Nicolls assumed the duties of Governor, New Amsterdam was changed to New York, and laws were enacted and courts established. Among the articles of capitulation agreed upon between Gov. Stuyvesant and Col. Nicolls, was the following, relating to the rights and privileges of the Dutch settlers:

"All people shall continue free denizens, and shall enjoy their lands, houses and goods, wheresoever they are within this country, and dispose of them as they please. The Dutch here shall enjoy their own customs concerning their inheritances."

By deed dated March 20, 1664, a portion of this territory (now New Jersey) was conveyed to Lord Berkeley and Sir George Carteret. The same day, they signed a constitution, which vested the government of the province in a Governor, and Council of Advice and Consent, and on the same date Philip Carteret was appointed Governor. He arrived in

July, 1665, and issued his Pronunciamento. He reorganized the court at Bergen shortly after, which was to be held and kept open as often as occasion required in the town of Bergen. The judges of this court were:

    NICHOLAS VERLET, Pres.,   HARMAN SMEEMAN,
    CASPAR STEIMMETS,   ILIAS MICHIELSEN,
                IDE VAN VORTS.

Chapter XVII.

BERGEN BECOMES AN ENGLISH COLONY.

The oath of allegiance was taken by the judges named in the last chapter, and also by the inhabitants of Bergen, on November 20, 1665 ; whereupon it became in truth an English province. This oath was as follows :

" You do swear by the Holy Evangelists, contained in this Book, to bear true faith and allegiance to our Governor, Lord, King Charles II., and his lawful successors, and to be true and faithful to the Lords Proprietors, and their successors, and the government of this province of New Jersey, as long as you shall continue a Freeholder and Inhabitant under the same, without any equivocation or mental reservation whatever, and so help you God."

In pursuance of the provisions of the constitution, the people were called upon to elect representatives to the Assembly, to be held at Elizabethtown, on the 25th of May, 1668 ; and on the 22nd day of September following, a new charter was granted by Gov. Carteret to the " Town and Freeholders of Bergen," and to the villages and plantations thereunto belonging, being in the province of Nova Cæsarea, or New Jersey.

" So that the whole tract of upland and meadow property belonging to the jurisdiction of the said

Town and Corporation of Bergen, is bounded at the north end by a tract of land belonging to Captain Nicholas Verlett and Wm. Samuel Edsall; on the east side by the Hudson River; on the south end by the Kill von Kull, that parts Staten Island and the main; and on the west by Arthur Kill Bay, and the Hackensack River." This included all the territory now known as Bayonne, Jersey City, Hoboken, West Hoboken and Weehawken, which was known as Bergen at that time, and was identical with the Indian grant to Gov. Stuyvesant, of January 20, 1658.

The Carteret Charter was a confirmation of the rights which the freeholders and the inhabitants of Bergen possessed under the Dutch domination. It confirmed to the freeholders " all the rights, immunities, and privileges hereby granted unto the said Corporation or Township," and gave them power to choose their own magistrates, or to be assistants to the president, or judge of the court, and for the ordering of all public affairs, within the said jurisdiction. It also made the following provision:—

" They shall have power to choose their own Minister for the preaching of the Word of God, and the administering of His Holy Sacraments, and being so chosen, all persons, as well the freeholders, as the inhabitants, are to contribute according to their estate, and proportion of land, for the minister, and the keeping of a free school, for the education of youth, as they shall think fit, which land being once laid out, is not to be alienated, but to remain and continue forever, from one incumbent to another, free from paying any rent, or any other rate of taxes; notwithstanding, it may be lawful for any particular person or persons to keep and maintain any other minister, at their own proper cost and charges.

"Also, power to divide all proportions of land, as are without their bounds and limits aforesaid, that are not already appropriated, and patented by particular persons, before the day of the date thereof, and compelling the recording of such allotments. And all mortgages, transfers, leases, and sales, for above the term of one year, and all other contracts, are to be void, and of no effect in law.

"That they shall have power to erect and ordain a Court of Judicature, within their own jurisdiction."

To encourage settlers, Carteret, after his appointment as Governor, 1664, issued an edict to the effect that every man who should embark with him, or meet him on his arrival, "provided with a good musket, bore twelve bullets to the pound, with bandelins and match convenient, and with six months' provisions" for himself, should receive one hundred and fifty acres of land, and a like amount for every servant or slave brought with him provided with the same necessities.

In 1672, war again broke out between England and Holland, and the Dutch fitted out an expedition for the purpose of destroying the English shipping, and attacking the settlements wherever practicable. The States General despatched a squadron of five vessels against New York, which arrived in July, 1673; and on the 30th day of that month they demanded the surrender of the fort at New York. This demand was acceded to, and the Dutch again took possession of the New Netherlands.

Chapter XVIII.

BERGEN BECOMES AGAIN A DUTCH DEPENDENCY.

Anthony Colve, captain of one of the vessels composing the Dutch squadron, was invested with the chief authority, and changed the name New York to New Orange; and a demand to surrender was sent to "the Village of Bergen, and the Hamlets and Boueries thereon depending," as follows:—

"You are hereby ordered and instructed, to despatch delegates from your village here to us, to treat with us on next Tuesday, respecting the surrender of your town, to the obedience of their High Mightinesses, the Lords States General, of the United Netherlands, his Serene Highness, the Prince of Orange, or on refusal to do so, we shall be obliged to constrain you thereto by force of arms."

The inhabitants of Bergen seem to have been no whit disturbed by this summons. Whether actuated by a loyalty to the old government, or restrained by the fear of losing their possessions, they surrendered without any attempt at resistance, and sent in the names of certain citizens, from which list a choice of magistrates could be made. The following were appointed on August 18, 1673, and required to take the oath of allegiance:—

SCHOUT AND SECRETARY, CLAES ARENTSE.
SCHEPENS.
GERRIT GERRITSE,   ELIAS MICHELSE,
THOMAS FREDERICKS,   PETER MARCELLESSEN,
CORNELIS ABRAHAM.

On the 21st of August they took the following oath: " Whereas we are chosen by the authority of the High and Mighty Lords, the States General, to be Magistrates of the Town of Bergen, we do swear in the presence of Almighty God, to be true and faithful to the said authority, and their Governors for the time being, and that we equally and impartially shall exercise justice between party and parties, without respect to persons or nations, and that we shall follow such further orders and instructions as we from time to time shall receive from the Governor and Council, etc."

They were thereupon notified that the Commander would visit their town on Sunday, after the sermon, in order to administer the oath to all their people. Pursuant to this notice the Commander and Council proceeded to Bergen, when the burghers of that town and dependencies were found to be seventy-eight in number, sixty-nine of whom appeared at drum beat, and took the oath of allegiance. The magistrates were ordered to forward the oaths of those who were absent.

On the 25th of August the authorities of Bergen were notified of the necessity of fortifying New Amsterdam, and that each community should contribute thereto according to its means. They promised such aid and support, and proceeded to organize a militia company, to prepare for such defence if needed. September 4, 1673, Caspar Stynmets was elected captain, Hans Diedrick lieutenant, and Adrien Post ensign.

The threatening aspect still continuing, on March 22, 1674, the authorities at New Orange ordered each of the Dutch towns within its jurisdiction to commission a militia officer and magistrate to meet at the City Hall, to confer on the state of the country; and it was then determined, in case of an enemy's approach, to send boats to Bergen to convey the people to the city.

Chapter XIX.

GROWTH OF BERGEN.

FROM the following report, dated 1680, we can gain a very correct idea of the growth and condition of the territory comprising "Old Bergen." "That there is a considerable settlement on Bergen Point, then called Constable Hook, and first improved by Edsall, in Nicoll's time; other plantations were improved along Bergen Neck to the east; between the point and a large village of some twenty families, further along lived sixteen or eighteen families, and opposite New York about forty families are seated southward from this. A few families settled together at a place called Duke's Farm (Aharsimus), and further up the country was a place called Hoebuck, formerly owned by a Dutch merchant who, in the Indian wars with the Dutch, had his wife, children, and servants murdered by the Indians, and his home and stock destroyed by them. But it is now settled again, and a mill erected there. Bergen is a compact town which had been fortified against the Indians, and contained about forty families. Its inhabitants were chiefly Dutch, some of whom had been settled there upwards of forty years."

The general condition of the territory may likewise be learned from the following extract from an

"Account of the encouragement for promoting a design of planting in East New Jersey," etc., in a letter from one George Scott at Edinburg, published in 1685, in which an allusion is made to the settlements and plantations of that time, in the territory now under consideration :—

"1st. Those on Overpeck Creek near Hackensack River, a river settled by several valleys, for which Mr. Nicolls, of New York, had a Patent, but gave leave to their settlement, at the request of Governor Carteret.

"2nd. Near to Snake Hill a piece of land almost an island, belonging to Mr. Penhorne, a Merchant of New York, and one Edward Eickbe.

"3rd. There are other plantations upon Hackensack River, which goes a great way up the country, almost northwest; others also on the east side of another Creek or River, at Hackensack River.

"4th. A large neck or tract of land, for which one Sarah Kiersted, of New York, had a Patent given her by an old Indian Sachem, in recompense for her interpreting the Indian language into Dutch, as there was occasion. There are some little families thereon; two or three miles up a great plantation, settled by Captain John Berry, whereon he now lives.

"5th. Another plantation adjoining belonging to his son-in-law, Michele Smith; another to Mr. Baker. This neck of land is in breadth, from Captain Berry's new plantation, on the west side where he lives, over to his old plantations, to the east at Hudson's River side, about three miles, which distance severs to Constable Hook, upward of ten miles.

"6th. To go back to the south part of Bergen Neck, that is opposite to Staten Island, where but a narrow passage of water, which ebbs and flows between the said Island and Bergen Point, called Constable's Hook, extending in land, above a mile over, from the Bay on the east side of the Neck, that leads to New York, to that on the west, that goes to Hackensack and Snake Hill, the neck running up between both, from the south, to the north of Hudson's River, to the outmost extent of their bounds. It was first settled by Samuel Edsall in Col. Nicoll's time and by him sold for £600.

"7th. Other small plantations along the neck to the East, are then named. Among them one to George Umpane (Communipau), which is over against New York, where there is about forty families, within which about the middle of the neck, which is here about three miles, overstands the town of Bergen, which gives name to that Neck. Then again northward, to the waterside going up Hudson's River, there lies out a point of land, wherein is a plantation and a water mill belonging to a Merchant in New York.

"8th. Southward there is a small village, about five or six families, which is commonly called the Duke's Farm. Further up is a good plantation in a neck of land almost an Island, called Hobuk. It did belong to a Dutch Merchant who formerly in the Indian War, had his wife, children and servants, murdered by the Indians, and his house, cattle and stock destroyed by them. It is now settled again and a mill erected there, by one dwelling at New York.

"9th. Up northward along the River side, are other lands near to Mr. William Lawrence, which is six or seven miles further. Opposite thereto is a plantation of Mr. Edsall, and above that Captain Bienfield's plantation. This last is almost opposite to the northwest end of Manhattan Island. Here are the utmost extent of the northern bounds of East Jersey as always computed."

Colve's reign was short, for on the 9th of July, 1674, the treaty of peace with England was concluded, which restored the whole country to the English. February 9, 1674, peace between Holland and England was established on favorable terms to the Dutch settlers, and the New Netherlands restored to English rule, which was continued until the Revolutionary War.

Sir Edmund Andros was commissioned Governor. He was recalled, and Thomas Dongan arrived on the 12th of August, 1683; the same year the first Colonial Assembly convened and adopted a Bill of Rights. On the conclusion of peace, the Duke of York obtained a new patent, similar to the first, dated June 29, 1674, and on November 6th of the same year, Governor Carteret published his Commission, and other documents at Bergen, in the presence of his Council. Commissioners were present from all the towns in New Jersey, except Shrewsbury.

It thus seems that Bergen was for a time the seat of government, and consequently may claim to have been the capital of the state. In 1682 the Province of New Jersey was divided into four counties; Bergen, Essex,

Middlesex and Monmouth. Bergen included all the settlements between the Hudson and Hackensack Rivers, and extended to the north bound of the province. In 1693 each county was divided into townships.

Chapter XX.

GROWTH OF BERGEN CONTINUED.

THOUGH the inhabitants of Bergen were now able to devote themselves to the improvement of their holdings, much dissatisfaction existed, not only because of the uncertain tenure and undefined boundaries of the land settled upon, but the "*out drift*," or common lands, were also a subject of controversy. The land considered as such, lying between Communipau and Bergen, caused much bickering, and although several agreements were entered into, they seem to have been only tentative. The cattle belonging to the two hamlets intermingling, and becoming thereby subject to adverse claims, were the cause of constant dispute. The feeling thereby became greatly intensified, and finally appeal was made to the authorities at New Amsterdam, whereupon the following order was issued:—

"May 24, 1674, the Schouts, Magistrates, and Commonalty, of the Town of Bergen, complaining by Petition that over two years ago, a question arose between the Petitioners and their dependent hamlets of Gemonepau, Mingaghun, and Pemropogh respecting the making and maintaining of a certain common fence, to separate the cattle, the Council at New Amsterdam ordered and commanded them to promptly regulate themselves, according to the decision or arbitration." This action on the part of the Council temporarily settled the difficulties, and the government of Bergen was continued under the Carteret Charter until 1714, when the land titles became again a subject of dispute, and new controversies arose. A petition was presented setting forth the facts in detail and praying for relief. January 14th, 1714, an act was passed giving the petitioners a new charter, under the name of "The Inhabitants of the Town of Bergen," giving full titles to lands, power to convey, etc., as follows :—

"It is agreed by, and between, all and every, the parties to these presents, that whatsoever part of the common and undivided lands, have been by them, or either of them, at any time heretofore taken up, used or claimed, and added to their patented, or purchased lands, shall forever hereafter, be deemed taken and adjudged, and shall remain and continue in common, until a division be made of the said common and undivided lands.

"Finally, for the faithful performance of these articles, they individually, bind themselves in the penal sum of One Hundred Pounds, proclamation money of New Jersey, to be forfeited and paid by any party breaking the agreement."

Signed by :—
MYNDERT GERRABRANTS.
CORNELIUS VAN NEWKIRK.
ABRAHAM DIEDERICK.
CORNELIUS K. GERREBRANTS.
JACOBUS VAN BUSKIRK.

Andries Van Buskirk.
Lowrens Van Buskirk.
Cornelius C. Blinkerhoff.
Michael C. Vreeland.
John Van Horne.
Ido I. Sip.
Jacob G. Van Wagener.
Jacob I. Van Horne.
Daniel Van Winkle.
Abraham Sickels.
Hendrich Van Winkell.
Johannis G. Van Wagener.
Johannis Van Houten.
Zacharias Sickelse.
Hendrich H. Spier.
Arent Taers.
Garret Roose.
Hendrick V. Siggels.
Cornelius Van Worst.
Jacob I. Brower.
Hendrick Vanderoff.
Lereymis Van Buskirk.
Sealed and delivered in presence of,
Johannis Vreelandt.
Dirck Kadmus.

June 16, 1743.

This agreement continued in force until December 7, 1763, when, in consequence of the impossibility of adjusting satisfactorily under its provisions the difficulties that were continually occurring, an act was passed by the General Assembly of the colony "for finally settling and determining the several rights, titles, and claims to the common lands of Bergen; and for making a partition thereof, among those who shall be adjudged, by the said Commissioners, to be entitled to the same." Under the operation of this act all feuds and controversies were ended, and the titles to lands made valid.

Peace prevailed throughout the settlement for some years, and its prosperity and growth continued until the breaking out of the Revolutionary War. The settlement of the territory of "Old Bergen" continued with considerable rapidity. Settlements sprang up at intervals, either because of some natural advantage or on account of a mercantile demand; people not only located along the shores of the bays and rivers almost surrounding the region, but also pushed back into the country, so that at the time of the Revolution, there were hamlets scattered from Bergen Point to the most northerly limits of the county. The inhabitants availed themselves of their opportunities to cultivate the soil, for the products of which they found an excellent market at New Amsterdam. Through their frugal and industrious habits they were enabled to increase the limits of their farms, until all the territory became the property of different settlers either as *buytentuyn* or wood lots. The winter months were employed in clearing these latter, and the timber cut down was placed on sleds and hauled to the home lot to be used for fuel.

As the growth of the town continued, new demands

were made for facility of intercourse. In 1669, Gov. Carteret appointed a new ferryman, reserving the right of free passage to himself and family, probably the first instance of the free pass system for officials in this country. In 1753, a road was laid out from Aharsimus by way of Prior's Mill to the church at Bergen, and intersecting it was a road along the line of Newark Avenue, across the marsh from Paulus Hook. This was often covered with water and frequently impassable.

As per following advertisement of July 2, 1764, in the *New York Mercury* of that date, there was " Good news to the Public ":——

" The long wished for ferry is now established, and kept across the North River from the place called Powles Hook to the City of New York."

This ferry was located at the foot of Grand Street, and was provided with an equipment of several row boats, with two oarsmen to each, with spare oars, so that such passengers as desired haste or exercise might be accommodated.

The same year, a stage route was established from this ferry, leading through Bergen Point, and thence by Blazing Star ferry to Woodbridge; whence passengers were conveyed to Philadelphia in covered wagons, the trips occupying two days in summer and three in winter. In 1767 a serious accident occurred on this ferry. While a coach containing passengers for Philadelphia was being ferried across, a number of passengers retained their seats; and when approaching the shore, the stage ran overboard, and two ladies were drowned.

As a road was laid out about the time of the starting of this ferry, running through about the present line of Grand, Warren, York and Van Vorst Streets, crossing the marsh and bridge at Mill Creek, following in a great measure the road to the mill before alluded to, and then connecting with the Old Mill Road, it is presumably the route by which this stage line passed through Bergen, thus corroborating the tradition, that the Old Mill Road was formerly the New York and Philadelphia Stage route. This is verified by the fact that one of the old residents informed the writer that through the cedar woods at that time standing along the brow of the hill, and about half-way between Montgomery and Mercer Streets, there was a lane cut through the hill which reached Summit Avenue, at a point south of present Montgomery Street, joining there a road that reached Bergen Avenue, at Foye Place; and that this was the New York and Philadelphia Stage route.

In 1765 the road leading to Brown's Ferry was laid out. This followed about the present line of Clendenne Avenue, and reached the Hackensack at a point south of the present Plank Road bridge. This ferry was afterward used as a connecting link for the lines of stages from Paulus Hook to Newark, and beyond. As the travel over this route, with the exception of the stage lines, was very infrequent, a horn was kept hanging on a tree near by, so that by a succession of blasts, the ferryman might be notified of the passengers' desire to cross. As showing the means of intercourse at this time between Newark and Jersey

City, the following advertisement is inserted : " Whereas the stage wagon from Newark to Paulus Hook, has for some time been stopt, for want of a proper person to drive the wagon through Bergen, the many complaints for the want of such a conveyance, induces the subscriber again to endeavor to accommodate them. He therefore proposes to drive through from Newark to Paulus Hook, once a day, every Monday, Tuesday, Thursday and Saturday."

It is probable that during the Revolutionary War all regular ferriage stopped, as we find that in 1786 an application was made to the Common Council of New York to repair the ferry stairs leading to Paulus Hook, which would indicate it was again in active operation. The Jersey landing at this time was at the foot of the present Grand Street. During the same period the ferry at Communipau was discontinued, but in 1783 the public was informed that Aaron Longstreet and Company gave " constant attendance by the Boats at the Ferry Stairs, near the Exchange (New York) at three p. m., to bring passengers to Communipau," where the Newark stage would be ready to convey them to Newark, and " thence by the excellent New York and Philadelphia running machines in one day to Philadelphia."

Chapter XXI.

REVOLUTIONARY TIMES.

But the peaceful existence of the inhabitants of "Old Bergen" was destined to be rudely disturbed. The demands and exactions of the English government seemed like a just retribution for the unjust treatment of the natives by the early Dutch authorities, for the colonists were thereby subjected to a similar experience. Mutterings of discontent grew loud throughout the provinces, and culminated in the open rebellion at Boston, followed by retaliatory measures on the part of the English government. A sympathetic feeling spread throughout the country, and the people of Bergen early became identified with the movement of the colonies for independence, as will be seen from the following extract from the proceedings of a meeting of the freeholders and inhabitants of the County of Bergen agreeable to advertisement at the Court House, June 25, 1774:

"The meeting being deeply affected with the calamitous condition of the Inhabitants of Boston, in consequence of the late Act of Parliament for blocking up the port of Boston, do

"Resolve that we think it our greatest happiness to live under the government of the illustrious House of Hanover, and that we will steadfastly and uniformly bear true and faithful allegiance to His Majesty George III. under the enjoyments of our constitutional rights and privileges.

"That we conceive it to be our indubitable privilege to be taxed only by our own consent, given by ourselves, or by our Representatives, and that we conceive the late Acts of Parliament, declarative of their rights to impose internal taxes on their subjects of America, as manifold encroachments on our national rights and privileges as British subjects, and, as inconsistent with the idea of an American Assembly, or House of Representatives," etc.

At this meeting delegates to attend a general Congress were chosen.

The early part of 1776 was a time of great anxiety for the colonists. Concerted action on the part of the several colonies had been determined upon, and measures adopted for resisting the enforcement of the demands of the mother country. The feeling of resistance became so much intensified that many outbreaks occurred, and as the patriotic movement crystallized, Bergen became the rendezvous of the American troops gathered from the surrounding country.

The Committee of Safety on March 26, 1776, announced as follows: "Considering the critical situation of the City and Province of New York, we do order and resolve that three Battalions of Militia be drafted out of the Militia of this Province, included in which are from Middlesex one hundred men, from Monmouth one hundred and forty men, from Essex two hundred and twenty men, from Bergen two hun-

"OLD BERGEN." 93

dred men, forming one of the Battalions. The whole to march to the City of New York with the greatest expedition."

Congress divided the southern and middle colonies into two Departments; New York, New Jersey,

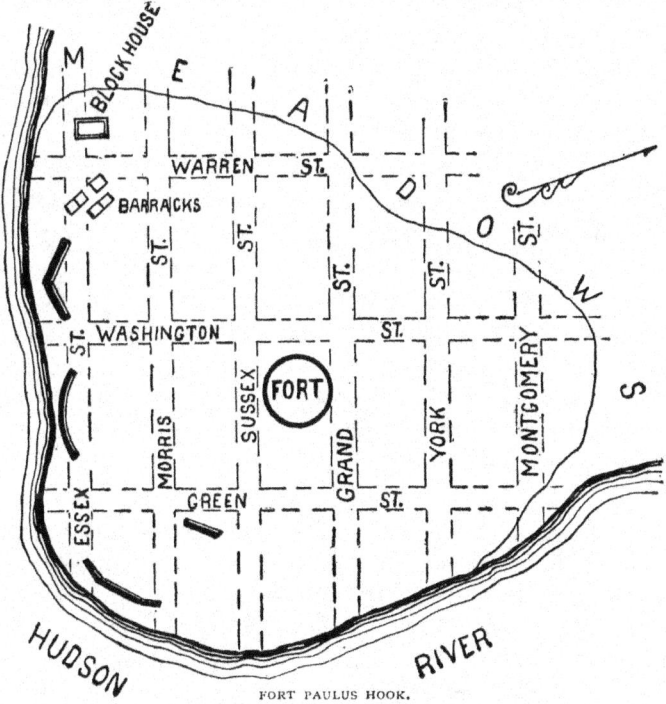
FORT PAULUS HOOK.

Pennsylvania, Delaware, and Maryland were to comprise the Middle, and Lord Stirling was given temporary command. In March, 1776, Gen. Hugh Mercer, a close friend of Washington's, and a veteran of Fort

Duquesne, joined the army, and was greeted by him with much warmth. The flying camp was just forming, and the Committee of Safety of Pennsylvania were forwarding some of their militia to the Jerseys. Washington at once gave command of it to Gen. Mercer, and sent him to Paulus Hook, to receive and organize the troops as they came in.

Lord Stirling, who was at this time in command of the American forces in New Jersey, recognizing the importance of holding this territory, ordered measures to be taken for placing Bergen in a state of defence. He counselled the building of forts at Paulus Hook, which would in a measure guard against attack from the Bay, and at the same time defend the approaches to the Hudson, and likewise ordered defences to be erected on Bergen Neck, to guard against any inroads from the southerly quarter. The fort at Paulus Hook was located on the high ground occupying the space now bounded on the north by Essex Street, and between Warren and Hudson.

The British fleet had left Boston, and its place of destination was unknown, although it was supposed to be New York. As it was hovering about this vicinity, great uncertainty prevailed as to the time and place of attack. This uncertainty was soon dispelled, for before the close of June, the enemy's fleet was descried nearing Sandy Hook, and as the ships approached the Staten Island shore, the troops commenced disembarking. They erected their tents, and encamped on the hills that sloped to the water's edge.

The Provincial Congress learned on the 29th of

June that nineteen sail of the enemy's fleet were at Sandy Hook, and forty-five in sight. Washington in a communication to Congress, July 4, 1776, from New York, says : " The enemy are already landed on Staten Island, and are leaving no arts unassayed, to gain the inhabitants to their side, and induce many to join them, either from motives of interest or fear, which I fear will be accomplished, unless there is a force to oppose them." The great aim of the British was now discovered to be to gain possession of New York City and the Hudson. Gen. Howe, writing to the home government, states: "We landed on this Island " (Staten), "to the great joy of a most loyal people, long suffering on that account, under the oppression of the rebels stationed among them.

"There is great reason to expect a numerous body of the inhabitants, to join the Army, from the province of New York, and the Jerseys, and Connecticut."

Shortly after landing on Staten Island, the British general stationed a small force, with two six pounders, on the extreme southeasterly point of Bergen Point, now called Constable Hook. The Americans, recognizing the danger of active operations being instituted by the British from this base, took precautionary measures to prevent their inroads. They strengthened the redoubt that was located on the high ground (near Forty-fifth Street and Avenue C) in Bayonne ; and July 4, 1776, Gen. Mercer was ordered to place there a garrison of five hundred soldiers, and likewise a strong guard at the ferries over the Hackensack and Passaic Rivers. Earthworks were erected on the heights of Bergen, east of Summit Avenue and near the line of Academy Street. As the need was felt of better facilities for the transportation of supplies, troops, etc., a good road leading from Paulus Hook to Brown's Ferry was projected, and also one from Weehawken to the northerly crossing of the Hackensack.

On the 12th of July, two vessels of the enemy's fleet, the *Phoenix*, forty guns, and the *Rose*, twenty guns, with their tenders, came up the Bay, and directed their course up the Hudson. The lookout on the Jersey shore, as well as that in New York, gave the alarm, and immediately all was activity. The batteries at Paulus Hook were freshly manned, and the priming of the already loaded guns was looked to ; and as the vessels came within reach, they were greeted with a tremendous cannonading. They sustained but little damage, however, as they were amply protected with sand bags ; and they passed on up, out of reach of shot, and anchored above Castle Point. The passing of these two vessels up the Hudson caused much anxiety, as it was feared that a landing of troops might be effected, which would not only harass and destroy the property bordering on the river, but might also cut off and capture the American troops stationed along Bergen Neck and Paulus Hook.

Chapter XXII.

REVOLUTIONARY TIMES CONTINUED.

On the evening of the same day great alarm was caused by a heavy cannonading down the Bay, and Bergen Heights were lined with patriots who were anxiously watching every movement of the enemy. It was discovered, however, that the great commotion was caused by the arrival of Lord Howe, who had sailed from England with reinforcements for his brother the general.

Meanwhile, matters were shaping themselves that ultimately led to the entire independence of the colonies. The Resolution of Independence, by the Continental Congress, was received by the New Jersey Committee, July 17th, 1776, and the following Preamble and Resolution were adopted:

"Whereas the Honorable Continental Congress, have declared the United Colonies free and independent states, We deputies of New Jersey in Provincial Congress, Resolve and declare, that we will support the freedom and independence of said states, with our lives and fortune, and with the whole force of New Jersey."

This action on the part of the state authorities cemented still more firmly the provincial forces, and they became more determined to resist the unjust demands of the mother country, pledging themselves to resist to the utmost, and oppose and destroy if possible, any force brought against them. Many projects were suggested to this end, and notable among them was one of Ephraim Anderson, adjutant to Second New Jersey Battalion, who conceived the idea of destroying the enemy's fleet in New York harbor, and submitted to Congress his plan for accomplishing it. It was favorably entertained, and Washington was instructed to aid him in carrying it into effect.

Anderson commenced at once the construction of fire ships, with which the fleet was to be attacked. At the same time an attack was to be made on the British camp on Staten Island, by troops from Mercer's flying camp, and others stationed at Bergen, under Major Knowlton. As Gen. Putnam was engaged in a plan for obstructing the passage of the enemy's ships up the Hudson at Fort Washington, he entered into this scheme with great ardor. He wrote to Gen. Gates: "The enemy's fleet now lies in the Bay close under Staten Island. Their troops possess no land here but the Island. Is it not strange that these invincible troops are so fond of islands and peninsulas, and dare not put their feet on the main? . . . We are preparing fourteen fire ships, to go into their fleet."

On the 31st of July, Anderson wrote to the President of Congress: "I have been for some time past very assiduous in the preparation of fire ships. . . . In my next I hope to give you a particular account of a general conflagration, etc." But he was disappointed, for it was not possible to construct a sufficient number of fire ships in time. Likewise, the recruits for the flying camp coming in slowly, the contemplated attack on the camp at Staten Island had to be abandoned. Still, a partial night attack was twice attempted by Mercer and Knowlton, but both failed.

The British army continued to gather, until at the beginning of August, there were in the vicinity of New York about thirty thousand men. On the 17th, Washington received word that three days' provisions had been cooked, and many of the troops had gone on board the transports, indicating that some important movement was to be undertaken.

At this time a gallant attempt was made to destroy the *Phoenix* and *Rose*—which had been threatening the shores of the Hudson since their passage up the river—by means of two of the fire ships. Although the attempt failed in its immediate object, one of the tenders to these vessels was burned, and the very daring of the attempt determined the commander of the vessels to join the rest of the fleet in the lower bay, and on the 18th of August, he made sail early in the morning and accomplished his purpose.

On the 21st, Brig. Gen. Wm. Livingston wrote Washington : " Having noticed unusual activity in the enemy's camp on Staten Island, I sent over a spy at midnight, who reported that twenty thousand men had embarked to make an attack on Long Island and up the Hudson, and that fifteen thousand had remained on Staten Island, to attack Bergen Point, Elizabethport and Amboy. The spy reported he had heard the orders and conversation of the Generals."

It can readily be imagined that the situation was deemed most grave. To discover and thwart the designs of the British commander now occupied the utmost energies of Washington and his generals; and from the shores of " Old Bergen " anxious eyes were continually peering through glasses to discover the first intimation of his purpose.

Likewise, the presence of the Tory or royalist element, who were quite numerous throughout the territory, made it necessary to exercise additional care and watchfulness, in order that they should be prevented from conveying to the enemy any knowledge of existing conditions, or of any intended movement of the patriots. Every endeavor was made to apprehend the disaffected, and prevent their communicating with the British.

At last the purpose of the enemy became evident. In the latter part of August, Clinton crossed the Narrows from Staten Island to Long Island, and the battle of Long Island shortly followed, resulting in the defeat of the American army, which withdrew to Harlem Heights, leaving New York City in complete possession of the English. This necessitated the greatest watchfulness on the part of the Americans at Paulus Hook, not only to prevent its capture, but because of the overbearing and aggressive action of the Tories among them, who were much emboldened by the success of the British arms. Consequently, stringent measures were adopted, and all the adherents of the royal cause were obliged to seek refuge in New York.

The following letter, dated August 8, 1776, was sent by the general commanding at New York to the president of the Provincial Congress in New Jersey: " I have received repeated information that a number of persons, known to be inimical to the cause of the American States, have removed to your State, and some very dangerous characters, lurking in the neighborhood of Hackensack, and what is called English Neighborhood, with intent, no doubt from its situation, of communicating with, and aiding our enemies. Urging stringent measures—as there is the greatest reason for believing, that the enemy intend to begin their operations in a very few days, and that with a very powerful force—you are urged to adopt effective measures, for furnishing troops and equipments."

During the active military operations above New York City, which culminated in the surrender of Fort Washington, November 16, nothing of any importance occurred within the territory of " Old Bergen," except the reception and assignment of troops, and constant watchfulness to guard against any sudden or unexpected movement on the part of the enemy.

Chapter XXIII.

REVOLUTIONARY TIMES CONTINUED.

IN September, 1776, Washington wrote to Gen. Mercer, of the flying camp, to keep a close watch on the movements of the enemy from the Jersey shore, and likewise to station videttes on the Neversink Heights, to make known at once if the British fleet should put to sea. He personally crossed over to Fort Constitution, afterwards named Fort Lee, a few miles above Hoboken, and extended his reconnoiterings down to Paulus Hook, to observe for himself what was going on in the city of New York and among the enemy's ships.

Gen. Greene now had command of all troops in the Jerseys, and was at liberty to make his headquarters at Basking Ridge or Bergen, as circumstances demanded, but was specially urged to at all times keep up communication with the main army on the east bank, so as to secure a safe line of retreat if necessary. He determined "to keep a good, intelligent officer at Bergen to watch the motions of the ships."

In an official letter dated September 16, 1776, Washington writes: "Yesterday at about 11 a. m., the British troops, under cover of a tremendous fire from eight or ten ships of war, effected a landing near Mr. Stuyvesant's house in the Bowery, and in a few hours took possession of the City of New York. About that time the *Asia* man of war, and two other ships, proceeded up the North River, but were roughly handled by the American battery at Powles Hook. This morning at daylight, the *Asia* came down much faster than she went up, she and her consorts having narrowly escaped destruction, by four of our fire ships that run in among them."

On the 23rd of September, part of the British fleet came up, and subjected the fort to a cannonading of over half an hour's duration. During this Mercer abandoned Paulus Hook, and withdrawing across the Hackensack, left a small scouting party at Bergen, with an advanced guard at Prior's Mill. A party of British was landed from the ships, and a force sent from New York in twenty boats, which took possession of the abandoned fort in the name of the king, immediately strengthened its defences, and held it continuously until the close of the war.

Bergen remained the headquarters of the American army until October 5, 1776. A letter dated October 4th says: "To-morrow we evacuate Bergen, as it is a narrow neck of land, accessible on three sides by water, and exposed to a variety of attacks in different places at one and the same time. A large body of the enemy might infallibly take possession of the place whenever they pleased, unless we kept a stronger force than our number would allow."

In October, 1776, while Washington and his army were at White Plains, two British frigates moved up the Hudson, with the intention of cutting off communication between Forts Lee and Washington. A battery on the cliffs at Fort Lee fired down upon them with but little effect. Two eighteen pounders were likewise brought down from Fort Lee, and planted opposite the ships. By the fire from both shores, they were hulled repeatedly, and General Green wrote: "Had the tide been flood one half hour longer, we should have sunk them."

The British army suddenly disappearing from White Plains caused Washington much uneasiness. On November 7, he wrote Gov. Livingston of New Jersey: " They have gone toward the North River and Kingsbridge . . . . I think Gen. Howe will make an incursion into Jersey." He recommended that the militia of the state be put on the best possible footing, and that those living near the water should be prepared to remove their stock, grain, etc., at the shortest notice. Information being received that Fort Lee was to be attacked, Washington directed Gen. Greene to have all stores not absolutely necessary for defence, immediately removed, and to destroy all supplies in the neighborhood which the owners refused to move, so as to prevent them falling into the hands of the enemy.

November 16, 1776, Fort Washington was attacked. Washington, with several of his officers, witnessed the battle from the heights above Fort Lee, and he saw with emotion the lowering of the American flag, that indicated its surrender. Realizing that Fort Lee would now be tenable no longer, he ordered all the stores and ammunition to be moved to a place of safety. This had been nearly accomplished, when it was learned that on the morning of the 20th about two hundred boat loads of British troops, under command of Lord Cornwallis, had crossed a few miles above.

They landed at Closter, six miles above Fort Lee, under the Palisades. Sir Wm. Howe states they " were obliged to drag the cannon up a very narrow road, for nearly half a mile, to the top of a precipice which bounds the shore for some miles on the west side." On receipt of such information, Washington, determining that the enemy's object was to extend their line across to the Hackensack, and thus entrap all the American forces below, gave orders for the abandonment of Fort Lee and the immediate withdrawal of all the troops. So great was the haste required, that much stores and most of the artillery were abandoned.

The retreat to the Hackensack commenced, and the American army succeeded in crossing the river safely, although they encountered the van guard of the enemy at the bridge crossing.

Chapter XXIV.

REVOLUTIONARY TIMES CONTINUED.

FROM its conformation, "Old Bergen" was untenable by the Americans after their defeat at Fort Washington, and the attack of the enemy on Fort Lee and its surrender. The British possessing full control of the waters that surrounded it on three sides, the danger was evident that by throwing any considerable force across the isthmus, their commander would effectually hem in and cut off all forces that might be quartered there. Consequently, Washington wisely withdrew his army, and continued his retreat across the Hackensack, camping at Hackensack from Nov. 19th to 21st, at Newark 23rd to 27th, at New Brunswick Nov. 30th to Dec. 1st, and at Trenton Dec. 3d to 12th. By this retreat East New Jersey was left in complete possession of the British, with the exception of a few scouting posts held temporarily by the Americans.

The heights of "Old Bergen," from their proximity to New York and their natural advantages, became the vantage ground of either side, as a place of observation, as well as a basis of operation, and Gen. Mercer was left in command of the flying camp at Paulus Hook for the purpose of reconnoitring. He kept there a small force, and was ordered to remain near the Hook and obtain what information he could, but to retire when threatened by the enemy. From its location and surroundings, the fort at Paulus Hook was well calculated to prove a secure outpost, through which the British were able to communicate directly with their headquarters in New York; and it was likewise well designed, as a base of operations, for any movement against the surrounding hostile country.

Built on a high peninsula, extending out into the bay, connected with the mainland by a narrow strip of sand, and otherwise surrounded by deep ditches, which could be artificially widened and deepened, and by almost impassable morasses, it is little wonder that it was in the continued possession of the British, throughout the whole of the Revolutionary War. From it, the enemy were able at all times to send out bodies of marauders to scour the country in search of booty or supplies, retiring in safety behind its defences, if surprised or threatened by superior forces.

The great importance of learning promptly of any contemplated movement of the British, caused General Mercer to station outposts along the heights of Bergen to watch for any indications of activity by the troops stationed in New York City. These scouts, concealed by the shadows of the woods and thickets with which the heights were covered, were enabled to approach unseen the brow of the hill, and from their elevated position gain important information that enabled the general to thwart the purpose of the enemy. "Old Bergen" was from this time forth the scene of active operations. Raids were frequent, and its inhabitants were at all times subjected to extreme privations. They saw their possessions in danger, and oftentimes their families were dispersed, and the fruits of their industry scattered. Patriots and Tories, with intermingled interests above and beyond a loyalty to a general government, that could in neither case guarantee safety and protection, were held between conflicting forces, and yet there were those in whose breasts the fires of patriotism burned brightly, and who, even in the darkest days, were ever true to the cause they had espoused.

The traditions of many of our families point to a self-sacrifice, endurance, and loyalty to the cause of liberty, unsurpassed in the annals of the country. Their houses were plundered, their grain and cattle seized, and themselves subjected to every indignity. This was the work not only of the Hessian hirelings, but frequently the British soldiers vied with them in their exacting demands. Likewise there were some who thought the rebellion foolhardy, and prompted by the desire of gaining favor with the British authorities, so as to retain their possessions, lost no opportunity of harassing their old neighbors. And yet sustained with the hope of eventually securing the independence to which they had pledged "their lives and fortunes," many of the inhabitants of "Old Bergen" suffered and endured, and even while overawed by the presence of hostile troops, eagerly seized every opportunity of affording assistance to the cause they had so much at heart.

The redoubt at Bergen Neck (Bayonne), called Fort Delancy, taken possession of by a party of refugees under Maj. Ward, was made the basis of many marauding operations against the Americans. Ward was a notoriously vicious character, and gathered about himself desperadoes and runaway slaves, who through their excesses and depredations, became greatly feared. Becoming involved in a financial difficulty with one of the neighboring farmers, he hired three of the negroes to kill him. They were seen and recognized, and were afterward hung in the woods northwest of Brown's Ferry (present Glendale) on Communipaw Avenue, about one quarter mile west of West Side Avenue.

On one occasion, when a detachment of the British were foraging from Paulus Hook, to protect themselves against the cold and storm, they took possession of a large barn of one of the old farmers of Bergen, located just west of Bergen Square and north of Academy Street, and built a large fire upon its clay floor. The owner, remonstrating with them, was seized, and would have become part of the fuel, had it not been for the intervention of an officer more humane than his comrades. However, they piled high the wood, which so increased the blaze that the structure was wholly consumed.

Chapter XXV.

REVOLUTIONARY TIMES CONTINUED.

IN recalling the history of the olden time, it must be remembered that there were those whose homes and everything they possessed were in this territory, and they naturally felt an unwillingness to jeopardize these if it could be avoided; and though with the exception of the capture of Paulus Hook, no battle of importance occurred within the territory of " Old Bergen," it was the general scouting ground for both parties. The territory was subjected to the worst of all forms of warfare; it had to endure not only the pillage of regular troops, but also the depredations of abandoned, irresponsible gangs, whose sole object was the booty they could secure, whether of friend or foe. Again, the disaffected from the neighboring country were transported thither, and thus added to the misery and sufferings of the inhabitants, as they were enabled to satiate their revengeful feelings on them. A few extracts taken at random will perhaps present a correct idea of the situation at this time.

June 30, 1777, Major Hayes, in pursuance of an order issued by Gov. Livingston, removed from the County of Essex certain women and children, and sent them on the east side of the Hackensack River.

July 1, 1777, a letter to the Governor from Newark

recites that the enemy had left Amboy and gone over to Staten Island and Bergen.

July 7, 1777, Gov. Livingston writes to General Washington : " By order of the Council of Safety, Gen. Winds has collected two hundred of our Militia, to proceed to the County of Bergen, under Major Hayes, to apprehend disaffected persons, and assist the Committee in securing, and disposing of, the personal estates of those who have gone over to the enemy."

July 19, 1777. "This morning the First and Second Pennsylvania Brigades, commanded by Brig. Gen. Wayne, marched from their respective encampments for the purpose of collecting, and bringing off, those cattle in Bergen County, immediately exposed to the enemy. After executing the order, Gen. Wayne on his return visited a Block House in the vicinity of Bergen Town " (probably the post commanded by Col. Cuyler near the Weehawken ferry, and mentioned elsewhere), " built and garrisoned by a number of Refugees, to avoid the disagreeable experience of being forced into the British sea service. The work was found to be proof against light artillery, when a part of the First and Second Pennsylvania Regiments were ordered to attempt to take it by assault. After forcing their way through the abatis and pickets, a retreat was indispensably necessary, there being no culrain into the Block House, but a subterranean passage, sufficient for one man to pass. The American loss consists of sixty-nine, including three officers, killed and wounded."

July 9, 1777, a letter was received by Gov. Livingston, complaining of the conduct of the Tory women, "as they secrete the goods, and conceal everything they can. When called upon for anything, they petitioned to leave, and go away Christians, and not be detained among brutes, as they call us. Pray make an order to send them among their Christian friends, our enemies."

August 26, 1777, the Governor and Council confined a number of disaffected inhabitants, chiefly of Bergen County; "to be released for an equal number of honest citizens stolen and imprisoned in like manner, to be determined in the future, thus to retaliate, till the enemy shall think proper to discontinue that infamous part of their infamous system."

Chapter XXVI.

REVOLUTIONARY TIMES CONTINUED.

GENERAL WASHINGTON to Gov. Livingston, Headquarters near Liberty Pole, Bergen County: " Our extreme distress for want of provision, makes me desirous of lessening the consumption of food, by discharging from this place as many as possible. Some brigades of the army have been five days without meat. To endeavor to relieve their wants, by stripping the lower parts of the county of its cattle, I moved two days ago to this place, and yesterday completely foraged Barbadoes, and Bergen Neck. Scarcely any cattle were found, but milch cows, and calves of one and two years old, and even these in no great quantity. When this scanty pittance is consumed, I know not to what quarters to look."

August 27, 1777, Washington writes to the Governor : " It has been no inconsiderable support of our cause, to have had it in our power, to contrast the conduct of our army with that of our enemies, and to convince the inhabitants, that while their rights were wantonly violated by the British troops, by ours they were respected. This distinction must now unhappily cease, and we must assume the odious character of the plunderers, instead of the protectors, of the people, unless very vigorous and immediate measures are taken by the State to comply with the requisitions made upon them."

Gov. Livingston wrote December 21, 1777: " I am afraid in furnishing clothing to our Battalions, we forget the County of Bergen, which alone is sufficient to supply them amply with winter waistcoats, breeches, etc. It is well known, that the rural ladies in that part of New Jersey pride themselves on an incredible number of petticoats, which, like house furniture, are displayed by way of ostentation, for many years, before they are decreed to invest the fair bodies of the proprietors. Till that period, they are never worn, but neatly piled up, on each side of an immense escritoire, the top of which is decorated with a capacious brass-clasped Bible, seldom read.

"What I would therefore most humbly propose to our superiors, is to make prize of these future female habiliments, and after proper transformation, immediately apply them to screen from the inclemency of the weather those gallant males who are fighting for the liberties of their country; and to clear this measure from any imputation of injustice, I have only to observe, that the generality of the women in that county, having for above half a century, worn the breeches, it is highly reasonable that the men should now, especially on so important an occasion, make booty of the petticoats."

The success of the American arms at Trenton and Princeton, and the practical hemming in of the British army in the extreme eastern part of the state, encouraged the patriots to renewed activity, and Washington, in urging the necessity of prompt forwarding of supplies and reinforcements, writes: "There is now a fair opportunity offered, of driving the enemy entirely from the Jerseys, or at least to the extremity of the Province." In most parts of New Jersey the people, exasperated at the treatment they had been subjected to by both British and Hessians, were resorting to arms; and the situation of the British army becoming more difficult, in the latter part of January, Sir William Howe crossed to Staten Island with his troops, and again occupied the old camping ground on the Bay of New York.

In the fall of 1777, the reinforcements awaited by Sir Henry Clinton arrived in New York Bay, and there were evidences of some important, combined movement designed by him. There was a great uncertainty as to its object, and Washington urged especial care and watchfulness, to prevent any unexpected movement. He sent scouts to the heights of Bergen, Weehawken and Hoboken, to be stationed at points which would command a view of the bay and river, to observe the situation of the enemy's forces, and note whether there were signs of an expedition up the Hudson, the occurrence of which Washington at all times strove to prevent.

In the fall of 1780, the revelation of the treachery of Arnold and the capture of Andre, created a great sensation in both the American and British lines. The base treachery of the former, together with the manly, courtly bearing of the brave but unfortunate Andre, created a desire for the capture of Arnold, and a hope that Andre might escape punishment. Captain Aaron Ogden, an officer of the New Jersey troops, was selected by Washington to bear a letter from Andre to Sir Henry Clinton. He was to take it to Paulus Hook, and from thence was to be conveyed across the river to New York. Captain Ogden was instructed to ascertain from the officer commanding at that post, whether Sir Henry Clinton might not be willing to deliver up Arnold in exchange for Andre. On his arrival at Paulus Hook, Captain Ogden, in the course of conversation, alluded to such possibility.

The officer demanded if he had any authority for making such a proposition, and Ogden replied: "I have no such assurance from General Washington, but I am prepared to say that if such a proposition were made, I believe it would be accepted, and Major Andre set at liberty." The officer crossed the river before morning, and submitted the matter to Sir Henry Clinton, but he rejected it, as incompatible with honor and military principle.

Chapter XXVII.

REVOLUTIONARY TIMES CONTINUED.

It was Washington's determination, if possible, to secure possession of the person of Arnold, and in an interview with Major Lee, he said: " I have sent for you in the expectation that you have in your Corps, individuals capable and willing to undertake an indispensable, delicate, and hazardous project. Whoever comes forward upon this occasion, will lay me under great obligations personally, and in behalf of the United States, I will reward him amply. No time is to be lost . . . . The timely delivery of Arnold to me, will possibly put it into my power to restore the amiable and unfortunate Andre to his friends."

A plan was formulated, and Maj. Lee selected John Champe, a young Virginian about twenty-four years of age. It required the utmost urging on the part of Lee to secure his assent to the plan, not because of fear of the danger to which he might be exposed, but because he was deterred " by the ignominy of desertion, and the hypocrisy of enlisting with the enemy." At last his scruples were overcome, and he entered upon the enterprise with all his native enthusiasm.

He was to make a pretended desertion to the enemy at New York, and there he was to enlist into a corps which Arnold was raising, and at a favorable moment in the night was to seize him, gag him, and bring him across the Hudson into Bergen Woods. Sergeant Champe's pretended desertion took place on the night of October 20. Besides stationary guards, he had to evade patrols of horse and foot, as well as irregular scouting parties, and so was obliged to proceed with great caution. At about eleven o'clock, taking his cloak, valise, and orderly book, he succeeded in mounting his horse and starting out. Shortly after, an alarm was sounded, that a dragoon had evaded the guard and escaped. The matter was reported to Major Lee, through whose instrumentality the affair was to be carried out. He was compelled to order out a pursuing party, under Cornet Middleton, but he contrived so many hindrances, that it was over an hour before the party could get off. The remainder of the incident is described by Major Lee as follows:

"Ascending an eminence before he reached the Three Pigeons, some miles on the north of the village of Bergen, as the pursuing party reached its summit, Champe was descried not more than a mile in front.

"His intention was to gain the British Post at Paulus Hook, but noticing his pursuers at about the same time they discovered him, and realizing that they would divine his purpose, he changed his route, and determined to seek protection from two British galleys lying a few miles to the west of Bergen. Entering the village, Champe turned to his right, and disguising his change of course, as much as he could

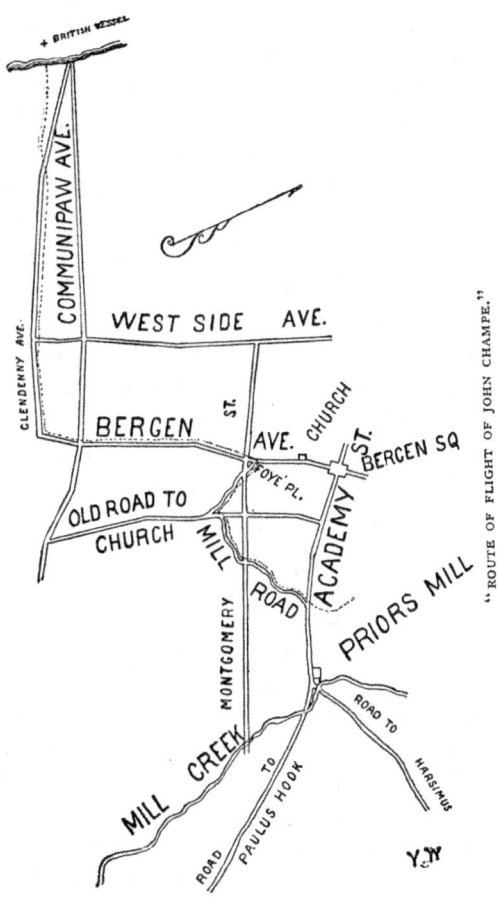

by taking the beaten streets, turning as they turned, took the Road toward Elizabethtown Point.

"His pursuers coming up shortly after, inquired of the villagers of Bergen, whether a dragoon had been seen that morning, ahead of his party. They were answered in the affirmative, but could learn nothing satisfactory as to the route he took. At last his trail was discovered, and followed so rapidly that they soon drew near. He lashed his valise containing his clothes and orderly book, on his shoulders, and drawing his sword, threw away the scabbard. The delay occasioned by these preparations, brought his pursuers within two or three hundred yards. He then dismounted, and running through the marsh to the river, plunged into it, calling for help. The galleys fired on the pursuing party, and sent a boat to meet Champe, who was taken on board and carried to New York."

Champe in his flight passed through Bergen Woods, and intending to reach the fort at Paulus Hook, directed his course along the easterly brow of the hill, and reached the vicinity of Prior's Mill. Finding himself cut off, he followed a lane leading up to the Mill Road, striking it just south of Academy Street; and continuing along the same, he came to Bergen Avenue at Foye Place; thence passing through Bergen Avenue, down to the neighborhood of present Clendenny Avenue, he took the road to Brown's Ferry, at the Hackensack, in the neighborhood of which he was rescued by the British boats.

Champe's successful evasion of his pursuers and

reception by the enemy, made it appear as if the plan would be successful. He enlisted in Arnold's corps, and arranged to surprise him at night, in a garden in the rear of his quarters. Champe's intention was to secure Arnold, while he was indulging in his usual evening walk, gag and bind him. By the removal of several pickets from the garden fence, he secured direct access to a boat, lying in wait near by. He was then to be taken across the Hudson and delivered into the hands of the American general. On the appointed night, Lee and three dragoons, with three led horses, were in the woods of Hoboken, waiting to receive the captive, but to their great disappointment no boat approached, and the Major and his companions were obliged to return to the camp.

The failure was afterward explained by the fact that the day preceding the date fixed upon, Arnold moved his quarters to superintend the embarkation of his troops (consisting chiefly of American deserters), among whom was Champe, whose plans were consequently foiled. He was unable to make his escape, and resume his real character for a long time. When he did so, he was amply rewarded by the Commander in Chief; and received the admiration and respect of his companions in arms.

The winter of '77 and '78 was of unusual severity, and even among the British army occupying New York City were its rigors felt. Fuel became scarce, and the wooded shores of "Old Bergen" were liberally levied upon. They furnished in great measure the fuel that was imperatively demanded to prevent suffering from cold. Many of the refugees, and those who were lukewarm, seized upon the opportunity to obtain some of the British gold in exchange for the timber they transported to the city. At Weehawken there was a natural gorge, which can still be seen in part, that afforded easy access to the water. Down its declivity, the logs were rolled to the water, and then towed across the river. There was likewise a similar ravine just above the West Shore ferry, that was used for like purposes. The scouting parties of the Americans discovering this, interfered with the traffic so successfully that the British erected a block-house at the head of the pass, to protect the wood-choppers. This was occupied by a detachment under Col. Cuyler, and was the scene of many conflicts until 1782, when it was abandoned and the garrison transported to Fort Delancy on Bergen Neck. This gorge was likewise taken advantage of by the runaway slaves from Bergen, who crossed to New York City in such numbers that an order was issued by the commander of the forces in the city, to Col. Cuyler, that he must prevent their crossing as they had become "such a burden to the town."

Chapter XXVIII.

REVOLUTIONARY TIMES CONTINUED.

ANOTHER incident deserving of mention, was the capture of the fort at Paulus Hook in 1779. The intense sufferings and privations of the American army at Valley Forge almost disheartened the most sincere patriots, and filled all hearts with gloomy forebodings. The great-hearted, faith-inspiring example and energy of Washington alone prevented the dissolution of the American army, and made possible the after events that checked the tide of despondency, inspired the struggling colonies with new hope, and foreshadowed the final triumph of a righteous cause. The battle of Monmouth as the result of his genius, the capture of Stony Point through the dashing bravery of the impetuous Wayne, and the overpowering and capture of the British garrison at Paulus Hook, through the shrewd foresight and daring intrepidity of Light Horse Harry Lee, were three events that deserve to be classed together, as among the most brilliant and important that occurred during the whole war.

It is hard to understand why an enterprise, considered at the time of so great importance, should be scarcely alluded to in our school histories. Washington wrote: "The increase of confidence which the army will derive from this affair and that of Stony Point, though great, will be among the least of the advantages resulting from these events." He also sent a special communication to Congress, commending Lee's remarkable degree of prudence, address, enterprise and bravery. Congress in full assembly, echoed the eulogy of the commander in chief, and ordered a gold medal, suitably inscribed in commemoration of the event, to be presented to Major Lee, a distinction which no other officer below the rank of general received during the war. Brevet rank and pay of captain were given to Lieutenants McAllister and Rudolph, and $15,000 in money distributed among the men, non-commissioned officers, and privates.

Lafayette in a letter to Major Lee says: "The more I have considered the situation of Paulus Hook, the more I have admired your enterprising spirit, and all your conduct in that business." James Duane, in a letter to Alexander Hamilton, characterizes it as "One of the most insolent and daring assaults that is to be found in the Records of chivalry, an achievement so brilliant in itself, so romantic in the scale of British admiration, that none but a hero, inspired by the fortitude, instructed by the wisdom, and guided by the planet of Washington, could by the exploit at Paulus Hook, have furnished materials in the page of History, to give it a parallel."

In Irving's *Life of Washington* we find the following graphic account of this exploit: "In the course of his reconnoiterings, and by means of spies, Major Lee discovered that the British Post at Paulus Hook, immediately opposite New York, was very negligently guarded. Paulus Hook is a long low point of the Jersey Shore, stretching into the Hudson, and connected to the main by a sandy isthmus. A fort had been erected on it, and garrisoned with four or five hundred troops, under the command of Major Sutherland. It was a strong position. A creek, fordable only in two places, rendered the Hook difficult of access. Within this, a deep trench had been cut across the isthmus, traversed by a drawbridge with a barred gate; and still within this, was a double row of abatis extending into the water. The whole position, with the country immediately adjacent, was separated from the rest of Jersey by the Hackensack, running parallel with the Hudson, at the distance of a very few miles, and only traversable in boats, excepting at the New Bridge, about fourteen miles from Paulus Hook.

"Confident in the strength of his position, and its distance from any American force, Major Sutherland had become remiss in his military precautions; the lack of vigilance in a commander soon produces carelessness in subalterns; and a general negligence prevailed in the garrison.

"All this had been ascertained by Major Lee, and he now proposed the daring project of surprising the fort at night, and thus striking an insulting blow 'within cannon shot of New York.' Washington was pleased with the project; he had a relish for signal enterprises of this kind. He was aware of their striking and salutary effect, upon both friend and foe, and he was disposed to favor the adventurous schemes of this young officer. The chief danger in the present case, would be the evacuation and retreat, after the blow had been effected, owing to the proximity of the enemy's force at New York.

"In consenting to the enterprise, therefore, he stipulated that Lee should not undertake it unless sure from previous observation, that the post could be carried by instant surprise. When carried, no time was to be lost, in attempting to bring off cannon, or any other articles, or in collecting stragglers of the garrison who might skulk and hide themselves.

"He was 'to surprise the post, bring off the garrison immediately, and effect a retreat.'

"On the 18th of August, 1779, Lee set out on the expedition at the head of three hundred men of Lord Stirling's division, and a troop of dismounted dragoons under Capt. McLane. The attack was to be made that night. Lest the enemy should hear of their movement, it was given out that they were on a mere foraging excursion. The road they took lay along that belt of rocky and wooded heights, which borders the Hudson, and forms a rugged neck between it and the Hackensack.

"Lord Stirling followed with five hundred men, and encamped at the New Bridge on that river, to be on hand to render aid if required. As it would be perilous to return along the rugged neck just mentioned, from the number of the enemy encamped along the Hudson, Lee, after striking the blow, was to push for Dow's Ferry on the Hackensack" (foot of present St. Paul's Avenue) "not far from Paulus Hook, where boats would be waiting to receive him.

"It was between two and three in the morning, when Lee arrived at the creek, which rendered Paulus Hook difficult of access. It happened fortunately that Major Sutherland, the British Commander, had the day before, detached a foraging party under Major Buskirk, to a part of the country called English Neighborhood (now Englewood). As Lee and his party approached, they were mistaken by the sentinel, for this party on its return.

"The darkness of the night favored the mistake. They passed the creek and ditch, and had made themselves masters of the fort before the negligent garrison were well roused from sleep. Major Sutherland, and about sixty Hessians, threw themselves into a small Block House, on the left of the fort, and opened an irregular fire.

"To attempt to dislodge them would have cost too much time. Alarm given from the ships in the River, and the forts at New York, threatened speedy reinforcements from the enemy.

"Having made one hundred and fifty prisoners, among whom were three officers, Lee commenced his retreat without tarrying to destroy either barracks or artillery. He had achieved his object, a 'Coup de main' of signal audacity. Few of the enemy were slain, for there was but little fighting, and no massacre. His own loss was two men killed and three wounded.

"Lee's retreat was attended by perils and perplexities. Through blunder or misapprehension, the boats which he was to have found at Dow's Ferry, on the Hackensack, disappointed him, and he had to make his way back with his weary troops, up the neck of land behind that river, and the Hudson, in imminent danger of being cut off by Buskirk and his scouting detachment. Fortunately, Lord Stirling heard of his peril, and sent a force to cover his retreat. Washington felt the great advantage of this hardy and brilliant exploit."

Chapter XXIX.

REVOLUTIONARY TIMES CONTINUED.

THE following letter, written by one of the officers actually engaged in this undertaking, is of interest. There seems to be a discrepancy between this account and that of Irving in relation to the number killed, as will be seen by comparison. In determining this, it should be considered whether Capt. Handy's position during the excitement of the engagement would allow him to make a positive or accurate report.

"Paramus, July 22, 1779.
" DEAR GEORGE :

"Before this reaches you, I doubt not but you have heard of our success at Paulus Hook, where the enemy had a very strong fort, within one and one-quarter miles from New York. We started from this place, on Wednesday last, at half-past ten o'clock, taking our route by a place called New Bridge, on the Hackensack River, where my two companies were joined by three hundred Virginians, and a company of dismounted dragoons, commanded by Capt. McLane.

"We took up our line of march, about five o'clock in the evening from the Bridge, the nearest route with safety to Powles, distant there, about twenty miles, with my detachment in front, the whole under command of the gallant Major Lee, the works to be carried by storm, the whole to advance in three solid columns, one of which I had the honor to command.

"The attack was to commence at half-past twelve o'clock, but having been greatly embarrassed on our march, and having a number of difficulties to surmount, did not arrive at the point of attack till after four o'clock in the morning, when after a small fire from them we gained their works, and put about fifty of them to the bayonet, took one hundred and fifty-seven prisoners, exclusive of seven commanding officers.

"This was completed in less than thirty minutes, and a retreat ordered, as we had every reason to suppose, unless timely, it would be cut off. Our situation was so difficult, that we could not bring off any stores. We had a morass to pass, of upwards of two miles, the greatest part of which we were obliged to pass by files, and several canals to ford up to our breasts in water.

"We advanced with bayonets fixed, pans open, and cocks fallen, to prevent any fire from our side, and believe me, when I assure you, we did not fire a musket. You will see a more particular account of it in the papers than I can give you at present. It is thought to be the greatest enterprise ever undertaken in America. Our loss is so inconsiderable, that I do not mention it."

(Signed)   LEVIN HANDY.

On the withdrawal of the American troops after this successful assault on the fort at Paulus Hook, great speed and caution were necessary to effect a safe retreat. The line of retreat intended was by the way of Prior's Mill and along Bergen Avenue, down to Dow's Ferry (about foot of present St. Paul's Avenue), it being Lee's intention to cross the Hackensack River, and join the main body near English Neighborhood. Capt. Forsyth was ordered to cover the retreat, and was stationed with a guard in the woods near what is now the junction of Bergen and Sip Avenues, with orders to remain there until Lee could reach the boats with his command. Through some blunder the boats had been removed, and Lee was forced to lead his weary troops over the rocky heights toward the main

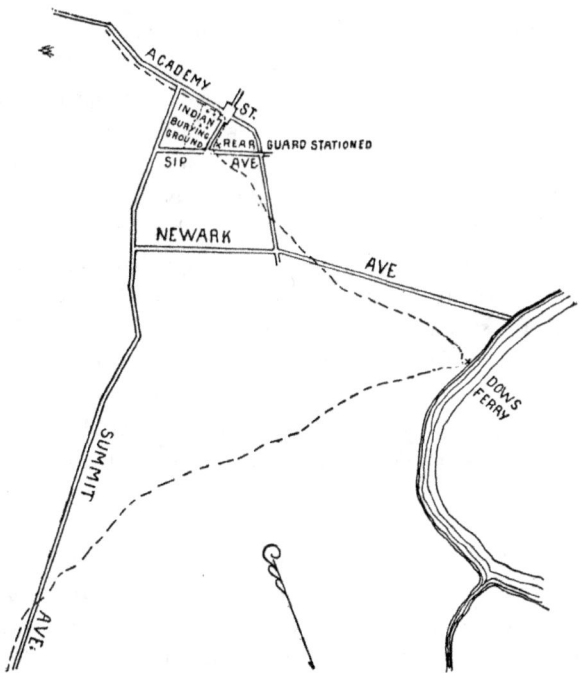

Map showing route of Lee's retreat in direction of Dow's Ferry and northward, and incidentally location of Old Indian burying ground, alluded to elsewhere.

camp; on ascertaining this fact Capt. Forsyth immediately followed, and by forced march caught up with Lee near the Fort Lee Road, where they met the escort sent to their assistance and reached the camp in safety.

During the winter of 1779 and 1780, the American troops were in quarters in the hills of Morristown, and were suffering great privations, being half fed and clothed, and subjected to the rigors of an unusually severe winter. New York Bay was solidly covered with ice of sufficient firmness to bear the heaviest artillery. Washington saw the opportunity, and determined to inaugurate some movement that would rouse the spirits of the people and inspire them with new hopes. He accordingly projected a descent on Staten Island with a force of two thousand five hundred men, under the command of Lord Stirling. His intention was to surprise and capture the British force stationed there. On January 14, 1779, the American force crossed to the Island from De Hart's Point, but their approach being discovered, and the British being strongly entrenched, they were obliged to recross to the Jersey shore, bringing with them, however, a number of prisoners who had been captured.

The boldness of this attempt roused the enemy, and on January 25th, Gen. Knyphausen ordered out a detachment, consisting of drafts from the different regiments stationed at New York, who passed over the North River in sleighs to Paulus Hook, and were there joined by part of its garrison. They crossed over Bergen Heights, collected what plunder they could, and pushing on to Newark, captured a company stationed there, and burned the academy.

In the beginning of October, 1780, Washington yielded to the urgent entreaties of Lafayette, and gave him permission to attempt a descent on Staten Island, to surprise two Hessian encampments. The attempt failed for want of boats. At the end of November, 1780, the New Jersey troops went into winter quarters in the neighhorhood of Pompton.

These were indeed trying times, and the fidelity and endurance of the patriots were tested to the utmost. Being exposed to the inclemency of the season without sufficient food and scantily clad, what wonder was it that stern necessity impelled to deeds of lawlessness that would not have been countenanced under other conditions, or that the rights of friend and foe were alike disregarded when ever personal advantage or comfort could be secured.

As an evidence of the actual condition of the patriot troops at this time, the following report taken from the *Royal Gazette*, dated August 26, 1780, will be of interest: "No man will now part with anything for paper money, old or new, and Washington's army, between Pompton and Tappan, are at three-quarters allowance of flour and fresh meat.

"At the late irruption of their light horse (about sixty) to Bergen, on Sunday 13th inst., they found the inhabitants going to church. Some they insulted, others they robbed, and condescended such pitiful exploits as changing hats and clothes, taking the buckles from their shoes, and in one instance stripping off a man's breeches, and leaving only an old pair of pants to cover his nakedness."

Although this is taken from a paper in full sympathy with the royalists, it would seem that Washington's prediction as to the change of policy from "protectors to plunderers" had been verified.

To show the value of Continental money at this time, the following bill is a fair sample:—

" 6 yds. chintz	$150	$900
1 pair boots	600	600
8¾ yds. calico	85	744
4½ yds. moreen	100	450
4 handkerchiefs	100	400
8 yds. binding	4	32
1 skein silk	10	10
		$3,136.

" If paid in specie, 18 pounds, 10 shillings."

Chapter XXX.

REVOLUTIONARY TIMES CONTINUED.

SIR HENRY CLINTON, persuading himself that South Carolina was subdued, embarked for New York on June 5th, 1780. On the 17th, the fleet arrived, and Clinton landed troops at Staten Island and then reëmbarked them, attempting to disguise his intention, which was to destroy the stores at Morristown and get control of the patriots' stronghold. In this he was thwarted, and commencing a retreat, he crossed into Staten Island on June 23rd, and New Jersey was at last evacuated by the enemy, with the exception of Paulus Hook.

(British Report, July 26, 1780.) "At a skirmish at Col. Cuyler's Post (near Weehawken), eight miles from New York, on the Hudson River, on Friday, 21st of July, three men were killed. The refugees under Capt. Ward pursued the rebels, and retook twenty head of cattle."

August 24, 1780, Lee with his command marched to the brow of the hill east of the town of Bergen (near Magnolia Avenue and Henry Street), took observation there of the movements of the enemy, and continued foraging as low down as Bergen Point.

(British Report, *New York Mercury*, August 28, 1780.) "Generals Washington, Lafayette, Greene and Wayne, with many other officers, and large bodies of rebels, have been in the vicinity of Bergen for some days past. They have taken all the forage from the inhabitants of that place. The officers were down to Prior's Mill last Friday, but did not seem inclined to make any attack."

The same paper states under date of September 18, 1780: " Four refugees that went over to Secaucus last Saturday, took three rebel officers and brought them to town yesterday morning."

Sir Henry Clinton, presuming on the disaffection existing among the Jersey troops on account of the privations and sufferings to which they were subjected, on January 4th, 1781, hurried troops, cannon and supplies of every description on board his vessels, so that he might land them on Staten Island, and then invading the Jerseys, encourage and take advantage of such disaffection. He found, however, that he had been deceived as to the actual sentiment of the American troops, and consequently failed in his object.

On July 1st, 1781, Washington received intelligence that a part of the garrison of New York had been ordered to forage the Jerseys. He therefore determined upon counter action, and he with some of his officers, crossed to Fort Lee to reconnoiter Fort Washington and the vicinity from the cliffs above. He found the troops that had been sent out into Jersey had been recalled in anticipation of some such movement, and he turned his attention to aiding in carrying out another part of the movement, the capture of Harlem Heights. About the middle of

July, Washington crossed the river with Count de Rochambeau, General de Beville, and General Duportail, to reconnoiter the British posts on the north end of New York Island. They were escorted by one hundred and fifty of the New Jersey troops, and spent the day on the Jersey heights, ascertaining the exact position of the enemy on the opposite shore. On the 21st of July, at eight in the evening, the troops commenced their march, and assumed so threatening an attitude that Clinton requested Cornwallis to send him three regiments to New York from Carolina.

After this reconnoissance, Washington urged reinforcements, and the French troops soon arriving (September, 1781), ground was surveyed and marked out on the Jersey shore (Bergen Heights), as if to aid in the siege of New York.

Washington now determined to attempt if possible the investment of New York, and in June took the field in person. He crossed from the western to the eastern side of the river, and was joined by the French army at Dobbs Ferry, July 6th. Clinton receiving a reinforcement of three thousand men from England, countermanded his requisition from Virginia. On consultation with the French commander, Washington determined to act in unison with him, and to dispose of the forces so as to move them most readily against New York or Staten Island, or, if deemed more judicious, to concentrate against Cornwallis.

Washington favored primarily the attack on Staten Island, as by its capture and possession by the Americans, the danger of an incursion up the Hudson would be greatly lessened. Sir Henry Clinton was in some way apprised of the design, and strengthened his corps in Staten Island and his post at Paulus Hook. Washington drew large bodies of his troops from the east side of the Hudson, and continued his offensive operations. All the boats that could be procured were collected at places convenient to Staten Island, and mounted on wheels ready for immediate transportation when required. The last division crossed the river on the 25th, assembling in the neighborhood of Paramus, preparatory to a forced march over Bergen Neck.

Washington here received a despatch from Lafayette, who was closely watching Cornwallis in Virginia, the purport of which decided him in favor of an immediate campaign against the latter. Necessary instructions were issued, and his army had actually crossed the Delaware before Clinton realized his real intention. It was Washington's design to mislead the British commander in case he decided to move against Cornwallis. Accordingly, pretended plans were drafted and allowed to fall into Clinton's hands; and to still further diminish the chance of his real design being made known, he gave orders for movements and operations that should mislead his own army. As he wrote, " No less pains were taken to deceive our own army, for I always conceived, when the imposition does not completely take place at home, it would never succeed sufficiently abroad."

Having thus completely outwitted Sir Henry

Clinton, Washington passed through Philadelphia, and eventually completed the movement that resulted in the defeat and surrender of Cornwallis. On his return he remained four months in Philadelphia, and then stopped at Morristown on his way to Newburg.

While here, a plan was submitted to him by Col. Matthew Ogden, of the New Jersey troops, to surprise Prince William Henry, son of the King of England, who was serving as a midshipman in the fleet of Admiral Digby, at his quarters in New York City, and bring both the prince and admiral off as prisoners. He was to be aided by a captain, a subaltern, three sergeants and thirty-six men. They were to embark from the Jersey shore on a rainy night, in four whale boats, well manned, and rowed with muffled oars, and were to land in New York at half-past nine, at a wharf not far from the quarters of the prince and admiral, which were in Hanover Square. Part of the men were to guard the boats, while Col. Ogden, with a strong party, was to proceed to the house, force the doors, and carry off the prisoners. Washington approved the plan, but Col. Ogden was specially charged that no insult or indignity should be offered the prisoners. It is not known whether any actual attempt was made to carry out this plan, but it was probably abandoned, as extra precautions were taken by the British at this time, on account of the many rumors and extravagant reports circulated in New York.

Chapter XXXI.

CLOSE OF THE REVOLUTION.

EVENTS were now rapidly culminating, and the long struggle for independence drawing to a close. The surrender of Cornwallis in October, 1781, virtually ended the war, although there were many skirmishes between detachments of the two armies, especially throughout the southern country, resulting in frequent bloodshed. The territory of Bergen still continued debatable ground, as will be seen from the following accounts:

(British Report, *New York Mercury*, September 17, 1781.) "On Wednesday evening last a party of eleven men under Capt. Wm. Harding, went from Fort Delancy on Bergen Neck, to Closter, and captured a rebel guard of six men and fifteen cattle, and took them safely to the fort."

(British Report, February, 1782.) "On Thursday morning before sunrise, a select body of rebels, consisting of some two hundred, from the Jersey Brigade of Light Infantry, aided by a party of picked Militia men, under the command of Maj. Bauman, attacked the post of Loyal Refugees at Bergen" (Fort Delancy at Bayonne), "commanded by Maj. Ward. . . . The rebels, who did not expect such a warm reception, were soon put in disorder, and obliged to change their position. They were formed in three columns on the ice, but the Refugees sallied out, and by a brisk fire from their small arms, and a nine-pounder served with grape-shot, did great execution, and obliged the rebels to make a precipitate retreat."

(British Report, *Royal Gazette*.) "On the night of the 13th inst., Capt. Geo. Harding, temporarily the commanding officer at Fort Delancy, having information that a party of rebels from Newark (who used to infest this shore and carry off our men) had gone over to Bergen Neck, detailed Capt. Cosman with a party of men to intercept them. The darkness of the night, however, favored the escape of the rebels."

(British Report, March 15, 1782.) "A party of Maj. Ward's Refugee Rangers, under command of Capt. Archibald McCurdy and Lieut. John Ferguson, made an excursion as far as English Neighborhood, in New Jersey, where they fell in with upward of fifty rebel Militia and Continentals. A skirmish ensued which lasted half an hour. The rebels were driven off."

The continued successes of the American arms, however, warned those who had been guilty of excesses, and who had been traitors to their country, that the day of retribution was at hand. Among the most active of these, were the band of refugees that had occupied Bergen Neck throughout almost the entire war. They now feared the vengeance of those they had so cruelly wronged, and "on the 1st of September, 1782, Fort Delancy on Bergen Neck was evacuated and burned; and on Saturday, October 5th, Maj. Ward, with his crew of Tories and Refugees, embarked for Nova Scotia, bearing with them implements of husbandry and one year's provisions."

Meanwhile negotiations for peace were being conducted at Paris. On the 20th of January, 1783, a treaty of peace was signed in that city, and on the 23rd of March, Congress received a letter to that effect from Lafayette, whereupon that body issued a proclamation announcing the fact, which was received by Washington on April 17th and read to the army on the 19th.

December 4th, 1783, Washington bade farewell to his officers at Fraunce's Tavern, Broad and Pearl Streets, in New York. A barge was in waiting at noon at Whitehall ferry to convey him across the Hudson to Paulus Hook, on his way to Annapolis, where he was to surrender his commission as commander in chief. As he approached the Jersey shore, the scene of so many anxious moments, he must have been affected by conflicting emotions. The contrast was marked. Only a few months had passed since the time when he could draw near to the shore only with the greatest caution. Now, he was welcomed with loud acclamation, the people of " Old Bergen " vying with each other in showing their love and admiration. He was hailed as the deliverer of his country, and many who, under his command, had endured and bled for their native land, invoked Heaven's choicest blessings on his head.

As he passed over Bergen Heights, his pride was mingled with sadness, as the surroundings revived in his mind recollections of former associates, his old companions in arms, whose dangers and privations he had shared, and many of whom had given their lives for the cause they loved. Among these was the gallant, self-sacrificing Mercer, whose faithful watchfulness from these very heights had aided so much in the result that had been attained, but whose life blood ebbed away, even as the turning point of the war was reached at Trenton and Princeton.

A few years afterward, when Washington received the reward of his labors and self-sacrifice through his selection as president of the infant confederacy, he again visited this scene of his early privations. On his journey to New York, on the occasion of his inauguration as first president of the United States, in 1789, his route was projected to pass through New Jersey to Elizabethtown Point, and then proceed by water to New York. His whole journey was in the nature of a triumphal procession, but nowhere was his reception more enthusiastic or his greetings more sincere than on his passage from the Point through the Kills. He embarked in a barge, splendidly decorated, and convoyed by others, with flags and music. As he entered the Kills, between Staten Island and Bergen Point, the procession was met by other boats from the shores, gay with bunting. From the shores of Bergen Point, which was lined with the citizens of "Old Bergen," he was greeted with the booming of cannon, waving of flags, and loud huzzas of the people. Their joy knew no bounds, and until the procession receded in the distance, their applause and rejoicing continued.

Says the general in his Diary: "The display of Boats which attended and joined on this occasion, some with vocal, and others with instrumental music, on board, the decoration of the ships, the roar of cannon, and the loud acclamations of the people, which rent the skies as I passed along the wharves, filled my mind with sensations as painful (contemplating the reverse of this scene) as they were pleasing."

Chapter XXXII.

GROWTH AND CHARACTERISTICS.

THE dangers and privations of the Revolution being now past, the people of Bergen once more resumed their avocations. Some there were who had cast in their lot with the British, and had been such active sympathizers with them, that they dreaded the retribution to which they would be subjected at the hands of their old neighbors, and failed to return. But the lukewarm and indifferent were permitted to occupy their old farms, and all now endeavored to rescue their lands and homes from the dilapidation and decay into which they had fallen. A few years sufficed to erase all traces of the bloody scenes that had been enacted, and the territory of " Old Bergen " resumed its accustomed quiet and peaceful appearance.

Many of the slaves now returned to their old masters, some actuated by kindly feeling, but most by self interest ; and their careless, irresponsible natures soon enabled them to assume their old relations, as if nothing had occurred to interrupt them. Their masters in many cases allowed them the privilege of cultivating small plots of ground after their regular working hours were over, and disposing of the proceeds of their labor for their own benefit; but through their natural improvidence, such benefit was but temporary, and oftentimes questionable.

The following extract is from a newspaper of 1804:

"At the Bear Market" (now Washington) "were seen on the Dock in the season for them, small stacks of cabbages, the perquisites, or overwork of the negro slaves from Hoboken, Paulus Hook and Communipau. They were brought over in canoes. After selling their stock, they would enjoy the jollification of a dance, upon the market floor, to the whistle of some favored one.

"They were very improvident, freely spending the proceeds of their hard labor, devoid of any care or solicitude, anxiety or forethought for the future, but perfectly contented and happy in the present."

The inhabitants of "Old Bergen" now devoted themselves in the main to the cultivation of the soil. The farms and truck gardens soon showed the effect of their vigorous and intelligent treatment. Sloop loads of produce were ferried over to New York, and many of the comforts of home, which had disappeared during the unsettled times, were again replaced. The increase in population demanding better facilities for communication, new roads were laid out, so that all parts of the territory could be readily reached.

The formation of Bergen town in the shape of a square, with the cross streets, has been described. One of these streets (Bergen Avenue) extended on the south, about on its present line, to Bergen Point, meeting the Old Mill Road at Foye Place, and crossing the road from Communipau at Harrison Avenue.

To the north it extended along what are now Sip and Summit Avenues, and beyond the Five Corners, into what was known as Bergen Woods. At the Five Corners, it intersected Newark and Hoboken Avenues.

Academy Street, another of the original streets crossing the square, extended on the west along present Tonnelle Avenue to what was called the Back Lots, now known as Homestead; and easterly to and along its present line, terminating abruptly at the rocks at Front Street, being opened through on its present grade in the early '50's. Summit Avenue ran from Academy Street south, as now, to Communipaw, being intersected below present Montgomery Street by the old Mill Road. The northerly section from Academy Street to Sip Avenue was opened more recently.

Until about the year 1848, when Grand Street was opened along its present line, the inhabitants of Communipaw and the lower end of the county were obliged to drive around through Bergen Avenue to Five Corners, and thence via Newark Avenue to the ferry; or take the Mill Road passing Prior's Mill. The latter route was, however, but little used, owing to the steep grade. Following the laying out of Grand and Montgomery Streets, the whole country was opened up so that transportation became comparatively easy in any direction.

Chapter XXXIII.

CHANGES.

IN 1789 the ferry landing at Paulus Hook was improved by the placing of steps, down which the passengers climbed, while horses and wagons were urged or lifted aboard the boats that served as means of transportation. This ferry connected with the stage route for Philadelphia, the proprietors of which built a tavern near Grand Street; and as the boats ran only between sunrise and sunset, the passengers were obliged to cross the river the night before, and consequently enrich the whilom host with the cost of the night's lodging and entertainment.

The following announcement was offered to the travelling public: " The wagons to be kept in good order, with good horses and sober drivers. They purpose to set off from Philadelphia and Paulus Hook on Mondays and Thursdays punctually at sunrise, and be at Princetown the same nights, and change Passengers and return to New York and Philadelphia the following days. The Passengers are desired to cross Paulus Hook ferry the evening before, as the wagon is not to stay after sunrise. Price, each Passenger from Paulus Hook to Princetown, 10s.; from thence to Philadelphia, 10s.; also ferriage free. Three pence each mile any distance between. Any gentlemen or ladies wanting to go to Philadelphia can go in the stage and be at home in five days, and be two nights and one day in Philadelphia to do business or see the market days."

In 1790 the Newark turnpike road was laid out, and over this after that date the Philadelphia stages wended their way. A considerable portion of the road from Jersey City to Newark was bordered on both sides by a thick-growing cedar swamp, which, being full of convenient hiding places, became the resort of thieves and robbers. Their depredations became so frequent, and the chance of apprehending them was so small, that in order to deprive them of this place of refuge, the whole tract was designedly burned.

It would seem, however, that previous to this time, a road existed leading to Newark via Belleville; for Brissot de Warville thus writes: " There is a causeway to Belleville built wholly of wood with much labor and perseverance, in the midst of water and soil, that trembles under your feet. It proves to what point may be carried the patience of man, who is determined to conquer nature." Another writer describes the delights of the journey as follows: "All the way to Newark (nine miles) is a very flat, marshy country intersected with rivers; there are many cedar swamps abounding with mosquitoes, which bit our hands and legs exceedingly; when they fix, they will continue sucking our blood if not disturbed, till they swell four times their ordinary size, when they absolutely fall off and burst with their fulness. . . . At two miles we cross a large cedar swamp; at three we intersect the road leading to Bergen, a Dutch town one-half mile distant on our right; at five we cross the Hackensack." The mosquito is evidently, from the contents of this letter, not a product of our present civilization, but existed even in those conservative days, and conducted his business with the same active aggressiveness as in more modern times.

The Duke de Rochefoucauld travelled over the road in 1796, and said it was very disagreeable to the traveller, being exceedingly rough, as it consisted of trees having their branches cut away, disposed longitudinally one beside another, and slightly covered with earth. In 1794 Henry Wansey, an Englishman on a visit to this country, wrote: "It" (this road) "is very convenient for those who live at Newark, and carry on their business at New York. Taking an early start on the 4th of June, I crossed Hudson's River to Paulus Hook to take the stage 'Industry' for Philadelphia, an hour and a half being required to make the passage; crossing the Hackensack, where a bridge was going to be built, to prevent the tedious passage by boat or scow, and the Passaic also, the coach and all in the scow, by means of pulling a rope which was fastened to the opposite side, we came to Newark." At this date, one stage sufficed for the transportation of residents of Newark who did business in New York, leaving Newark at six o'clock a. m., and returning from New York at three p. m.

In 1800 and for a number of years following, the only public conveyance of passengers by land between Newark and New York was by means of one two-horse stage coach, which went to Paulus Hook in the morning and returned in the evening. The road was extremely rough, and in wet weather almost impassable. In

1813 there were four stage lines between New York and Philadelphia: "The Pilot," leaving New York at 5 a.m., accommodating seven passengers, and arriving at Philadelphia next morning; "Commercial," leaving at 7 a. m., passengers remaining at Trenton over night and reaching Philadelphia next morning; "Mail," leaving at 1 p. m. and arriving at Philadelphia next morning at 6 o'clock; "Expedition," leaving New York at 4 p.m., stopping at Rahway, then at Burlington for the night, and arriving at Philadelphia the next afternoon.

Through the courtesy of Dr. L. J. Gordon, we are enabled to present an accurate cut of an interesting incident connected with early railroading, which, although not especially related to the general subject of this work, still clearly shows the small beginnings of our present magnificent transportation system. Much opposition to the proposed method of propulsion by steam was developed, and theories were demonstrated to show the impossibility of success. One objection advanced was that it was not possible for a locomotive to round short curves. In order to prove the fallacy of this claim, Peter Cooper built a locomotive, which he called "Tom Thumb," for practical experiment. It was tested on the Baltimore and Ohio Railroad Aug. 22, 1830. An extract from a letter written by H. B. Latrobe, brother of the chief engineer of this road, gives a graphic description of the event.

"I send you copy of my sketch of Mr. Cooper's locomotive and the horse-car. . . . The trip was most interesting. The curves were passed without difficulty

Exciting Race between Mr. Peter Cooper's Locomotive, "Tom Thumb," and a Horse-Car.

The trial took place on the Baltimore and Ohio Railroad, on the 28th August, 1830. The sketch represents the moment the Engine overtook and passed the Horse-Car, the passengers filled with excitement. (See Mr. Latrobe's description.)

at a speed of 15 miles an hour. . . . But the triumph of this 'Tom Thumb' engine was not without a drawback. The great stage proprietors of the day were Stockton & Stokes, and on that occasion a gallant horse of great beauty and power was driven by them from town attached to another car on the second track—for the Company had laid two tracks to the mills—and met the engine on its way back. From this point it was determined to have a race home. The start being even, away went horse and engine, the snort of the one and the puff of the other keeping time and time. At first the horse had the best of it, for his steam would be applied to the greatest advantage on the instant, while the engine had to wait until the rotation of the wheels set the blower to work. The horse was perhaps a quarter of a mile ahead, when the safety-valve of the engine lifted and the thin blue vapor issuing from it showed an excess of steam. The blower whistled, the steam blew off in vapory clouds, the pace increased, the passengers shouted, the engine gained on the horse. Soon it lapped him; the silk was plied, the race was neck and neck, nose and nose. Then the engine passed the horse, and a great hurrah hailed the victory. But it was not repeated, for just at this time, when the gray's master was about giving up, the band which drove the pulley which moved the blower, slipped from the driver, the safety-valve ceased to scream, and the engine for want of breath began to wheeze and pant. In vain Mr. Cooper, who was his own engineer and fireman, lacerated his hands in attempting to replace the band upon the wheel; in vain he tried to urge the fire with light-wood. The horse gained on the machine and passed it; and although the band was presently replaced, and steam again did its best, the horse was too far ahead to be overtaken, and came in the winner of the race."

The experience of the passengers on the early steam roads is told in a letter of Judge Gillis of Ridgway, Penn., describing his trip from Albany to Schenectady in 1831.

"The trucks were coupled together with chains or chain links, leaving from two to three feet slack; and when the locomotive started, it took up the slack by jerks with sufficient force to jerk the passengers, who sat on seats across the top of the coaches, out from under their hats, and in stopping they came together with such force as to send them flying from their seats.

"They used dry pitch-pine for fuel, and there being no smoke or spark catcher to the smoke-stack, a volume of black smoke, strongly impregnated with sparks, coals and cinders, came pouring back the whole length of the train. Each of the tossed passengers who had an umbrella raised it as a protection against the smoke and fire. They were found to be but a momentary protection, for I think in the first mile the last one went overboard, all having their covers burnt off from the frames; when a general mêlée took place among the deck passengers, each whipping his neighbor to put out the fire."

Chapter XXXIV.

TRANSPORTATION.

Up to 1832 the only means of rapid communication between New York and Philadelphia was by boat from New York to Amboy, and thence by rail, via Bordentown and Camden, to Philadelphia, with a spur from Bordentown to Trenton. Intercourse in this part of the state was carried on by means of stage lines, of which at that time there were twenty crossing Bergen territory for different points. But after that date the growth of the country and the demand for easy communication with the capital of the state required increased facilities.

March 17, 1832, the New Jersey Railroad and Transportation Company was incorporated, being designed to provide the then new facilities of railway travel between Trenton and New York, "and to restore the old Colonial and Revolutionary route over New Jersey, through Newark, Elizabeth, Rahway and New Brunswick, to Princeton and Trenton." Work was commenced, and the road laid out and completed, with the exception of the cut through Bergen Hill and the filling east of the "Point of Rocks" (now the site of the Penn. R. R. Round House on Railroad Avenue).

It must be remembered that there were at this

time no steam drills or other modern appliances for the removal of rock, and the excavation was a great undertaking. In order to lessen the work, and, as stated to the stockholders by John P. Jackson, the then president of the road, to save an expense of $100,000, the curve at the eastern end of the cut was adopted. It followed an old ravine or water-course, the direction of which may be seen from the Summit Avenue bridge. Before the roadbed was straightened by the Penn. R. R., about 1878, the road reached in a straight line from the ferry along the line of Railroad Avenue to just west of the "Point of Rocks," and thence turning sharply to the north, followed a graceful, S-like curve to a point near Marion. When the road was built, much difficulty was experienced in crossing the old Mill Creek, by reason of the nature of the marsh. So treacherous was the foundation it afforded, that although the roadbed was filled up to grade several times, all would sink and entirely disappear in a single night. While this tedious work was going on, cars were drawn by horses from Marion over the hill, making a trip each way every hour and a half during the day, and three trips during the night.

It is evident that the railroad magnates of the early days not only performed their own clerical work, but supervised very closely all matters connected with the conduct of the company's affairs, as the following extracts will show. These are taken from letters in their own handwriting, folded and sealed with wafers in the olden style, with superscription on back. They likewise indicate some of the difficulties connected with early railroading. "Jan. 22, 1836. When the train cars pass through Newark, they are to stop 5 minutes as advertised. The agents will regulate the time. In case, however, they have more than 5 minutes before the time advertised for their passing through Newark, they must hold over until that hour arrives." What a relief it would be to some of our dilatory suburbanites were this comfortable, easy-going system to prevail at the present time.

"Feb. 3, 1836. I enquire why our train stopped at Newark without going through. I hope you will pay attention to this, and as much as possible be there when the trains pass through, to see that things go right." In the early organization of the road and the irregularities naturally caused by its unfinished state, annoyances were continually arising from the want of a settled code of discipline. It must be remembered that at this time horse power was used to propel the cars over Bergen Hill.

"Feb. 5, 1836. As regards the trains to Rahway, you observe that the arrangement is made for the future, and that as soon as we run a locomotive to Bergen Hill, they have no more to do with Newark than with Elizabethtown. . . . For the present, I am desirous to have you see to their getting on properly, changing horses, etc." Another difficulty seems to have been in properly distributing the cars. "There is but one car here to go out at 11.30 o'clock. Please remember that the cars must not get all at one end, and that the two train cars must not go except in their trains. As there is but little business doing, why not have a portion of the cars at Jersey City?"

At this time wood was used exclusively as fuel, and was brought by vessel and unloaded on the unfinished wharf. "Feb., 1836. We have two loads of wood at Jersey City, one pile on the end of our bulkhead, and the other on the south ferry dock. If the ice is firm enough to have it carried ashore, it had better be done now." "Dec. 2, 1836.—— has sent word that he wishes to clean his pumps on Sunday. Please find out if it is absolutely necessary to stop, and if so, *send the mail by sleigh.*"

As showing the tremendous development of railroad traffic in this section alone, in a little over sixty years, the following advertisement, taken from the *Jersey City Gazette* of 1835, is of interest: "The Public is respectfully informed, that the N. J. R. R. is now open for public use between Newark and New York, and cars will commence running to-morrow, 8 trips each way daily, fare $37\frac{1}{2}$ cents, ferry to New York, $6\frac{1}{4}$ cents. New York and Easton Stages: Passengers will cross the river from foot of Cortlandt St. to Jersey City, then take Post coaches through Springfield, Chatham, Morristown, Mendham, etc., and arrive in Easton, same evening. Morristown stage will leave Newark, every day at half-past one o'clock, so that the passengers who leave New York in the morning, by the Hoboken Stages, the steamboat *Newark* at 10 o'clock, or the Rail-Road cars at half-past eleven, will be in time to dine at Newark, and take the stage for Morristown." Contrast this with the fact that from the Penn. Central R. R. Depot in Jersey City alone, above three hundred regular passenger trains arrive and depart every twenty-four hours, to which must be added freights and specials; while the Erie, Lackawanna and New Jersey Central roads each control a very large traffic.

The whole road from Philadelphia was finished, and engines operated the entire length, Jan. 1, 1839. At Marion the Paterson and Hudson R.R. terminated, and after the completion of the N. J. R. R., reached Jersey City by connecting with it at this point. The Paterson and Hudson was incorporated January 21, 1831, and went into operation in June, 1832. The rolling stock consisted of " three splendid and commodious cars, each capable of accommodating thirty passengers, drawn by fleet and gentle horses; a rapid and delightful mode of travelling." It was first operated by horse power, and when a change was made to steam, it must have been with many misgivings, for it was advertised that " The steam and horse cars are so intermixed that passengers may make their selection, and the timid can avail themselves of the latter twice a day." The old "Grasshopper Engine," with its walking beam, loping along like its predecessor—the running Indian—was in strong contrast with the present smooth-running, swiftly moving, intelligent iron steed.

This road was afterward absorbed by the Erie, and was the route by which that road reached tidewater at Jersey City, until the completion of the Erie Tunnel in 1861. This enterprise was a formidable undertaking, owing to the length of the cutting and the hardness of the trap rock through which it was bored. During the tunnel's construction considerable trouble was experienced with the workmen, which culminated in a serious strike and riot, necessitating the calling out of the militia.

It is stated that when the building of the New Jersey Railroad commenced in 1833, Cornelius Van

GRASSHOPPER ENGINE.

Vorst was so incensed that he offered to sell the whole of his possessions for $1,000. (*His. Soc. Proceedings.*)

We can scarcely realize in this era of trolley development, that but little more than forty years ago, the one-horse stage of old Peter Earle met all the demands for local travel in Bergen. But he combined within himself motorman, conductor, superintendent, yes, and directors too, for he " scooped " all the dividends.

He made one trip each way daily, to accommodate his regular passengers, of whom there were four, J. J. Franks, F. P. Vidal, George Gifford and Prof. House. In case any other service was needed, or the ladies wished to visit the bargain counters of the day, notice had to be sent him the night previous. Passengers were required to be in readiness at 10 o'clock in the morning, when he would call for them, with the understanding that they would be at the ferry at 3 o'clock in the afternoon to return home, so that he might have time to go back for his regulars, at 5 o'clock.

After a time, two more emigrants settled in Bergen, which necessitated the procurement of a two-horse stage, with seats for eight. With these vehicles, Earle was able to accommodate the travelling public until Jacob M. Merseles—to whose foresight and energy the town owed much of its development—anticipating the rapid approach of a demand for more and better conveniences for travelling, purchased the Pioneers, and started his omnibus line, which ran from the stables at Montgomery and Orchard Streets and followed the route of the Newark Avenue line of cars to the ferry. Shortly after, one Hallock started another line, but after a few weeks of fruitless opposition, sold out to Merseles, who incorporated the Bergen Stage and Plank Road Co. He found the roads at certain seasons of the year almost impassable, and wisely united the Stage and Plank Road Companies, so that the stages could have the benefit of the road without extra cost. The plank road was laid along Bergen Avenue from Communipaw to Newark Avenues, and a toll-gate was maintained at the Summit Avenue bridge.

This stage line was afterward merged into the Jersey City and Bergen Horse Car Co. The first cars operated on this road were in the shape of the old omnibus body, fastened on the truck by a pivot in the center, and drawn by one horse. They were most convenient for swinging around at the end of the route, or in case of meeting between switches, but required constant watchfulness on a descending grade, lest inadvertently the car should get before the horse. A few years ago electricity was applied as a motive power, and the original line swallowed up by that electrical octopus, "The North Jersey Traction Co."

Chapter XXXV.

CHURCH AND SCHOOL.

RELIGION and education were considered of the utmost importance by the early Dutch settlers, and the church and school in the primitive days were very closely united, and under the control of the same governing body. Indeed, in most cases, the schoolhouse was built first, and served the double purpose of a place of instruction, and a house for church service. The great anxiety of the sturdy colonists was to perpetuate the faith of their fathers, and to procure means for the instruction of their youth.

For several years, the village of Bergen possessed the only organized church community on the west side of the Hudson, and people came from far and near to worship there. According to Dr. Taylor, the first building was a log structure, which was used for divine worship for eighteen years. As it is well authenticated that the octagonal stone church, mentioned hereafter, was erected in 1680, it follows that this first rude building must have been erected in or before 1662. According to the deacons' accounts, the building needed considerable repairs during the years 1678 and 1680, at which dates there are several entries of expenditures for nails and labor, for nailing boards on the schoolhouse, etc., indicating a somewhat advanced state of dilapidation. Hence the year 1662 may be considered as the date when the attempts of the early settlers to establish a church, were crowned with success.

In that year we likewise find the following petition in the records of the Council: "The Schepens of the Village of Bergen, having observed and considered the fatherly direction and care of your Hon. Worships, in erecting church and schoolhouses, they request that they may have a God-fearing man, and preacher to be an example to, and teach the fear of God in, the Community of Bergen, and its jurisdiction. They state that the inhabitants now pay of their own free will, a yearly contribution of four hundred and seventeen guilders, in wampum, and would do more. They therefore think that your Noble Honors should send one over at your own expense, for one or two years, until the land should so increase in value, that the good-hearted could liberally give."

Just when and where the first church or schoolhouse was erected, it is impossible to state positively, but it would seem from this petition, that at least one, or perhaps both, were in existence at this date, as the chief anxiety of the people seems to have been to procure a minister from the Company. Tradition says that the first church services were held in the building—probably the schoolhouse just alluded to,—located at the northeast corner of the old graveyard (near the corner of Tuers Avenue and Vroom Street), and the bulk of testimony corroborates this. The divine service of the day was without much doubt held there until the erection of the church in 1680. We learn from the records of the deacons of the church showing the collections taken, that church services have been maintained regularly at least since 1667. There seem to be no records in existence, of occurrences previous to that time. Oftentimes, as opportunity offered, some of the people would cross over to New Amsterdam, to attend the services held there in the Dutch church, although facilities were given them for divine service at home.

In 1680, the people decided to begin the erection of their first church building proper, and on May 23, 1681, the dedicatory sermon was preached by Rev. Casper Van Zuren, from Long Island. The collection taken up on this occasion amounted to eighty-seven guilders and ten stivers, or nearly forty dollars of our money. The church was a stone building, octagonal in shape and was located near the corner of Bergen Avenue and Vroom Street. It was surmounted by a brass rooster for a weathercock, which was transferred, on the demolition of the building in 1773, to the spire of the edifice that succeeded the "little church" at that date; and in 1841 when this second church was in turn pulled down, the vane was placed on the cupola of the Columbian Academy. In the early '50's, a gunner returning from his day's sport, perhaps in an exhilarated state, and imagining he had discovered a rare kind of game, levelled his gun at the old weathercock, and damaged it to such an extent that it was taken down and repaired with iron braces. It was then replaced, but soon the action of the weather

166   "OLD BERGEN."

again weakened it, and a well-directed stone from the hand of an ambitious youngster completed the work of destruction. One of the old residents in the vicinity of Bergen Square had a facsimile of the original made and placed on the present School No. 11, where

TYPE OF OCTAGONAL CHURCH.

it still remains to mystify onlookers as to the direction of the wind.

In the interior of the old church, seats were placed around the wall for the male worshippers, while the women occupied high-backed chairs, which were their personal property. Some of these chairs are still cherished as heirlooms by the descendants of their original owners. In the winter season, the foot-stove was carried to and from service, and this was a very necessary companion, for otherwise there were no facilities for producing artificial warmth. It was a small box of wood, perforated, and containing a metal cup, in which the owner before leaving home, placed hot embers, making it a most acceptable footstool.

The minister declaimed from a pulpit placed high above the congregation and surmounted by a sounding board, and at the end of his sermon admonished the deacons to collect the contributions of the people. For this purpose they used black velvet bags with bells attached and fastened to long poles, and by a judicious jingling, awakened not only the sleeping faculties of the drowsy ones, but it is hoped likewise their consciences.

The *voorleser* occupied a position in front of and below the pulpit, from which he performed the services in the absence of the preacher, or led the singing at the regular services. For over ninety years the congregation was without a stated pastor; the voorleser, or schoolmaster, conducting the services on the Sabbath, which consisted of prayer, and reading a sermon prepared by one of the ablest theologians in the Fatherland. During the occasional absence of the voorleser, different members of the church performed his office; and at intervals, when ministers from different parts of the country happened to be at New York, they crossed the river to preach to the Bergen people. The names of the Revs. John and Samuel Megapolensis, Wilhelmus Niewwenhuysen, Caspar Van Zuren, Henricus Selyns, Gualterus Dubois, G. Bertholf, W. Lupardus, B. Freeman, of Schenectady; R. Erickson, A. Curtenius, Cornelius Van Schie, of Fishkill; J. Leyt, George W. Mancius, H. Marinus, and others, appear in the deacons' books of accounts; for the preachers were always remunerated for their services.

Besides expenses and board, they received from twenty-five to seventy-two guilders per service. As is shown by the accounts, the ministers coming from New York were obliged to pay six guilders to the ferryman, and six guilders for a carriage from the ferry to Bergen. Cornelis Brinkerhoff was for years the person who discharged the duty of transporting the ministers; while upon the Van Houten family rested the responsibility of providing sustenance and lodging for them, an expense of twelve guilders, seawant, being charged in the deacons' accounts after each visit. The amounts mentioned above were paid in wampum. This was obtained by the deacons from the authorities, and by them sold to the heads of the families composing the congregation; when collections were taken, this was dropped in the bags (a guilder equalled 20 stivers, a stiver an English penny).

In 1679, the people agreed with the minister of the City, meaning New York, to administer the Lord's Supper three times a year, for which he received thirty bushels or fifteen bags of wheat. He performed this service on week days, because he could not be absent from the city on Sunday, as he was the only minister. In the same year twelve guilders were expended in the purchase of printed sermons, and December 31, 1682, the consistory authorized the purchase, for the sum of seventy-five pounds, of four large theological works, with the following titles: *The Secret of Happiness in God*, *On the Epistles to the Philippians*, *Explanation of the Catechism*, and *The True Repentance*.

A "sand runner" or hour-glass stood on the desk in the church, and when the sand had run out of the upper part, the reader was obliged to suspend services, and dismiss the congregation. Engelbert Stuynhuysen (afterwards mentioned as schoolmaster) appears to have been the first voorleser, and served in that capacity from October, 1662, until about 1664 or 1665, when Reynier Bastiase Van Giesen was called upon to officiate in his stead. He continued therein for about forty-two years, and was followed by Adrien Vermeulen, who served for twenty-eight years, and on April 3, 1736, he was succeeded by P. Van Benthuysen, who filled the office for just twenty-five years, until April 3, 1761. Abraham Sickles was then appointed, and was the last of the voorlesers of "Old Bergen," serving until 1789, when a "clerk" was appointed, at a salary of two pounds, fifteen shillings, per annum.

The voorleser, besides receiving a salary for that office and as schoolmaster, was likewise paid for his services as bookkeeper and *aansprekcr*, and perhaps received some token from the people for special services, as at marriages and baptisms.

Rev. Henry Selyn wrote to the Classis of Amsterdam from New York, October 28, 1682 : "At the request of the people of Bergen, I have consented to preach there, three times a year, on Mondays both morning and afternoon, and administer the Lord's Supper. I found there a new church, and one hundred and thirty-four members. At other times, they are accustomed to come over the River here, to the hearing of the Word." Arrangements were made with Mr. Selyn to officiate at regular intervals, and he commenced his services October 2, 1682, and continued to perform his duties faithfully until 1699. Other ministers, however, officiated on the Lord's Day during this time. In 1699 Rev. Gualtherus Dubois became a colleague with Mr. Selyn in the church at New York, and he thereafter performed the services in the Bergen church for more than half a century. September 2, 1700, he dispensed the Lord's Supper, and continued his ministrations until 1751.

DR. DUBOIS.

Chapter XXXVI.

THE CHURCH.

IN 1750, the congregation, feeling their need of a stated pastor, determined to use their utmost endeavors to secure one. They arranged with the church on Staten Island to extend a joint call to one who should minister to the two congregations, and finally extended a call to one Petrus De Wint. In his call, the conditions were specified as a "righteous half of services and a righteous half of payment," as he was to minister to the two churches, of Bergen and Staten Island. The church at Bergen was to furnish him with firewood and a parsonage, and that at Staten Island was to give him "an able riding horse with all that belongs to it." As, under the church rules, it was necessary for this call to be approved by the Classis at Amsterdam, it was forwarded there for endorsement. Meanwhile he commenced his labors, but was never installed, as a response was received from Holland, stating that De Wint was an impostor, having presented forged credentials. He was therefore discharged June 23, 1752. This experience caused the congregation to exercise great caution in their subsequent endeavors.

On the 22nd of June, 1753, a call was extended to William Jackson, who was at that time studying at

Raritan. By the terms of this call, he was required to go to Holland to prosecute his studies, and be regularly ordained by ·the Classis of Amsterdam. During his absence, he was to be paid one hundred pounds by the churches calling him. He accepted this call, with the conditions; and sailing for Holland, remained there for nearly four years. On his return he was installed in the church at Bergen, September 10, 1757. To show their appreciation of the services of a minister, and their recognition of the obligations they had voluntarily assumed, the congregation had prepared a parsonage for him, so that he might be relieved of any anxiety concerning temporal matters.

December 20, 1771, the church was granted a charter by the English Crown, and incorporated under the name of "The Minister, Elders and Deacons," as follows:

REV. WILLIAM JACKSON, MINISTER.

Elders.
{ ABRAHAM DEDRICHS.
ROBT. SYCKLES.
GEORGE VREELAND.
ABRAHAM SYKLES. }

Deacons.
{ HENDRICUS KUYPER.
JOHANNIS VAN WAGENEN.
JOHANNIS VAN HOUTEN.
DANIEL VAN WINKLE. }

They were empowered to appoint a clerk, schoolmaster, bell ringer, etc. Thus we see that at every opportunity, and with every advance, the cause of education was brought forward prominently, and fostered with great care. In 1773 the church accommodation was found inadequate to meet the wants of the growing congregation, and a new building was erected on the same site. As the accounts of expenditures connected with this building are incomplete, it is impossible to state just when the first services were held, or

OLD CHURCH.

when the building was completed. From May 17 to October 17, 1773, about three hundred and sixty pounds had been expended for material and labor.

Dominie Jackson was an uncompromising patriot, and during Revolutionary days his open and emphatic support of the cause of liberty did much to strengthen its advocates, and prevent the wavering from openly espousing the side of its enemies. So open was his denunciation of King George and his supporters, that he was arrested and taken under guard before Lord Howe, in command at New York. He there admitted the charges brought against him, but justified himself by insisting that he simply performed his duty according to the dictates of his conscience. He was released, and permitted to return to the scene of his labors.

He ministered unto the congregation with much acceptability, until there were indications of mental disturbance, and his faculties failing; the two churches requested that they be relieved from the obligation of their call, and be permitted to call a new minister. The church at Bergen secured to him, however, the use of the parsonage they had built for him, during his natural life, together with four acres of land adjoining, and probably the church on Staten Island likewise made some provision for him.

The great inconvenience being recognized of attempting one pastorate over these two churches, they being so widely separated, arrangements were made by the churches at Bergen and English Neighborhood for uniting in a call to some minister who could acceptably meet the wants of the two growing congregations. Consequently, on the 28th of November, 1792, they made a joint call on John Cornelisen, who accepted and entered on his ministry. Until this time, all the services in the Bergen church had been rendered in the

Dutch language, and the church register was continued in the same until 1809.

By the terms of his call, Dominie Cornelisen was to preach in Dutch at Bergen on Sabbath mornings, while at English Neighborhood he was required to preach in that language only occasionally. When he was officiating at the latter place, the voorleser conducted the services at Bergen.

Chapter XXXVII.

CHURCH CONTINUED.

THE old parsonage, on the site of the present church, and before alluded to, being in possession of the Rev. William Jackson, in 1793 the consistory purchased the Sip homestead, in the town of Bergen, situated on the northwest corner of the Square. The house was of stone, of the antique model, long, low, and only one story in height, the window frames on the exterior being surmounted with ornamental brick work. Mr. Cornelisen occupied this building from the time of his marriage until his death. It was then raised to two stories in height, and otherwise improved. The lot on which it stood contained two acres, part of which is now the property of Mr. Geo. B. Wilson.

The care of this large parish, extending from Bergen Point to within three miles of Hackensack, a distance of eighteen miles, was soon found to be too much for a single clergyman, not only on account of its great area, but also because of the growth of both congregations. The duties of the pastor multiplied greatly, and it became evident that a separation must be effected. The interesting account of Prof. Demarest, of the conditions and experiences of the early congregations, is specially applicable here.

" I would that I could give an authentic account of

OLD PARSONAGE.

the church-going habits of these people" (English Neighborhood) "during their connection with the church of Bergen. Doubtless they were all in attendance, on every Communion Day, whether it were the Lord's Day or Monday.

"They would make all their preparations on Saturday, or the day previous, so that they might start early in the morning, for the distance was nearly twenty miles, the roads not macadamized, the wagons springless, and the farm horses not very fleet. Besides, it was desirable to have, after so long a journey, a half hour's rest before the service, for the good of body, mind and soul.

"The proximity of the Inn to the church, customary in those days, was not an unmixed evil. Perhaps after the services, some Van Horn, or Van Winkle, or Van Riper, Van Wagenen or Vreeland, would insist on taking the company home to dinner, for nothing pleased the Dutchman of that day so well, as to have his table crowded on a Sunday, by people whom he respected. Sometimes very little of the day, especially in the winter, would be left after the close of public worship, for the Communion Service occupied hours; and then they would tarry till morning, and on the Monday wend their way homeward.

"They were not so driven and hurried in their worldly business as men now are. Perhaps they often brought their lunch with them, and having been refreshed by it, started on their tedious journey for home, which they would not reach until after nightfall. We may well believe, too, that the forests through which they passed, in going to and returning from the house of God, were made to ring with the psalms of Marot and Beza."

It was at last deemed judicious to dissolve the bond that united these two churches, and on November 21, 1806, the consistory at Bergen arranged for the entire services of the pastor, and on December 1, issued a new call to him. The next day this was approved by the Classis, whereupon the connection was dissolved, after an existence of fourteen years, and Dominie Cornelisen assumed entire charge of the church at Bergen. He was to receive $450 yearly, "together with the parsonage, and a lot of land, containing about thirty-two acres, the building and fences to be kept in good repair; also thirty loads of fire-wood, forty bushels of grain, and three free sabbaths each year."

From this time Mr. Cornelisen's labors were confined to Bergen, and he was obligated to perform his services in Dutch and English on alternate sabbaths. He was a man who enjoyed the full love and confidence of his people, and as was the custom in the olden days, his advice and counsel were much sought after and heeded. He considered the colored people under his charge (at that time slaves), as committed specially to his care and protection. He instructed them in religious truths, and a number were admitted to church fellowship. During his ministry, the church services changed from Dutch to English. Singing in Dutch was first discontinued in 1809. Preaching in that language continued some time later. The history of his ministry is one of continuous growth, and great acceptability to his congregation. He died March 20, 1828, and Benjamin C. Taylor was called on the 26th of May the same year, and installed July 24.

Chapter XXXVIII.

LATER HISTORY OF THE CHURCH.

AT this time there were in what is now the County of Hudson, three churches, the Reformed Dutch in Bergen, the First Presbyterian Church in Jersey City, and a small Methodist Church at Five Corners. St. Matthew's Episcopal congregation worshipped in the old Town Hall, then used for school purposes, and located near the site of its present building in lower Jersey City.

The congregation of the First Presbyterian Church previous to this had worshipped in the old Town Hall for some years, but losing their pastor (Rev. Mr. Olcott), they determined to become a Reformed Dutch Church; by a unanimous vote they decided to unite with the Bergen Classis, and on the 16th of February, 1830, the church became thus duly constituted. The property on Grand Street, now occupied by the Free Reformed Church, which had been deeded by the Jersey Associates to the First Presbyterian Church of Jersey City in 1828, became thereupon the property of the Dutch Church.

But soon a demand arose for increased church accommodation, and the community began to discuss the propriety of the erection of other houses of worship. As the population increased and settlements were formed in the outlying territory, it was determined to erect churches in such localities as to accommodate, to a great extent, those families who lived at a distance from the mother church. Hence Dutch churches were established at Jersey City in 1807, and Bergen Neck in 1828 ; and as the demand continued, these were followed by others. Nor was this the only church growth. As there were many gathering within the territory belonging to other denominations, the need was felt for suitable accommodation for them; and from time to time, in accordance with the demand, other churches were established, until at the present time the confines of " Old Bergen " are studded with the spires of churches belonging to every denomination. Dr. Taylor was closely identified with what might be called the formative period of Old Bergen. When he commenced his ministry, the habits and customs of the Fatherland prevailed to a very great extent, and the rustic population dwelt apart from the follies and vices of the neighboring city, in genuine old Dutch simplicity. He lived, however, to see many changes effected, and the beginning of many of the improvements and advancements which he predicted, and which have transformed

DR. TAYLOR.

the country garden into town lots, and the quiet, staid farming community into a busy, bustling city.

That the "Faith of the Fathers" has been kept in all its purity, is not surprising, when it is considered

PRESENT REFORMED CHURCH, BUILT 1841.

that it was incumbent on the minister to present once each Sabbath, some portion of the Articles of Belief. As this was divided up, according to the Heidelberg Catechism, into fifty-two "Lord's Days," every year the congregation were regaled with a complete discussion and review of the tenets of the faith, and were thereby strengthened and confirmed in its doctrines.

During the pastorate of Doctor Taylor, the present church edifice was erected (in 1841). The original church parsonage stood on this site, for July 12, 1841, the consistory "Resolved that the old parsonage be taken down to make room for the new" (the present) "church edifice, and that the building Committee use the materials to the best advantage they can." During the erection of this church building, the Columbian Academy was secured for Sabbath morning worship, the teacher agreeing to vacate the second story for the sum of $5 per quarter. Just south of the church, convenient and substantial sheds were built, for the protection of the horses of those who lived at a distance and still adhered to the "Old Church;" while the tavern, but a few feet further south, was resorted to by some, during the interval between the services, for their noonday meal.

Doctor Taylor continued his active pastorate until the infirmities of advancing age made "the grasshopper a burden." The consistory recognizing his failing physical powers, declared him "Pastor Emeritus," and issued a call to the Rev. James L. Amerman, who was installed May 7, 1871. A remarkable degree of mutual confidence and

REV. JAMES L. AMERMAN.

sympathy existed between these two, and thus were happily combined the buoyancy and strength of youth, with the wisdom and experience of age. What might be called the joint administration of the two clergymen continued as long as the "Old Dominie" was able to actively coöperate. He died Feby. 2nd, 1881. Doctor Amerman continued to minister faithfully to his congregation until June 1st, 1876, when, feeling that he was called to perform active, personal missionary work among the heathen, he was at his own request dismissed, and became a missionary to Japan.

He was followed by the Rev. Doctor Cornelius Brett, who was installed August 1st, 1876, the church being without a regular pastor only two months, June and July. He still continues his pastorate, having ministered faithfully and acceptably to his people for over a quarter of a century. He presents the faith of the Fathers in all its purity and simplicity; yet recognizing the change of conditions, he preaches rather the doctrine of love than that of retributive justice.

REV. DR. CORNELIUS BRETT.

Chapter XXXIX.

CHURCH CUSTOMS.

THE church has always exercised special care of the poor, and the contributions for that purpose have been liberal. About 1675, the expense of the Poor Fund was so small proportionately, that there existed a considerable surplus. Whereupon, that the fund might not diminish, but rather show somewhat of an increase, the surplus was invested in cows, which were placed in the charge of responsible members of the congregation, at a yearly butter rent of twelve pounds of butter, or its equivalent in money. In 1679 the price of butter was so high that thirteen guilders and four stivers rent was received from one cow, something over $6, or an average price per pound of butter of over fifty cents.

After 1715, the deacons quit the butter business, and confined themselves to money-lending as a means of increasing the revenue; and we find that people for miles around came to Bergen to borrow money. This was given on proper bond, or on receipt and custody of sufficient personal property. The fund was also increased by collections taken at weddings, and on special occasions, such as birth-days, recovery from sickness, etc.

"On Wednesday, November 6, 1678, Siebe Epkse (Banta) and Maritze Aryanse Sip, were united in marriage, in the Village of Bergen, by the voorleser; collection 2 florins, 19 stivers." This entry occurs in the deacons' book, showing that collections for the poor were, sometimes at least, taken up at weddings. As the currency of the day was mostly in seawant or wampum, the receipts and expenditures were calculated from that standpoint. An English pound was worth forty florins, seawant; an American dollar was worth eight florins.

Another singular source of revenue was the renting of the pall. This was used to cover the coffin, and was owned by the consistory, and rented out as required on funeral occasions. The first pall was procured in 1678, and was used on the occasion of the burial of Engelbert Stuynhuysen, the cost of which is specified in the deacons' accounts, as follows:

 10 El. of Black Cloth, at 24 g. per El., 240 guilders.
 A linen cover to protect the pall, 14 "
        Total, 254 "

An entry December 25, 1711, shows that the receipts for the use of the pall to that time amounted to 864 guilders and 17 stivers, or $352.40 of our money. We find, however, that notwithstanding the utmost care, the Deacons' Fund was at times subjected to losses; borrowers died bankrupt, and securities, as now, depreciated in value, and there is in the hands of the church treasurer a large amount of money of Colonial and Continental issue.

In the early days, as was usual in many rural communities, family burial plots were located in some convenient part of the farm, and the territory was dotted with the little enclosures, made sacred to the memory of the dead.

But soon after the custom was established of burying church members, especially, in close proximity to the church, which doubtless accounts for the existence of the old cemeteries at Tuers and Bergen Avenues and Vroom Street, as the old churches were located on these two plots; and it became the recognized custom to perform most of the burials there.

An itemized account of the expenses incurred at a burial in 1690, not only informs us of the cost of such ceremony, but suggests something of the customs of the day.

Coffin and spirits,	25 g., 10 st.	Aanspreker,	19 g., 10 st.
½ Keg of Beer,	15 g., 16 st.	Carting the goods,	3 g., 00 st.
Flour and Milk,	6 g., 5 st.	Sundries,	15 g., 05 st.

Total, 85 g., 06 st.

The aanspreker was an official whose services were absolutely necessary, at all well regulated funerals in the Fatherland, and as the early settlers retained and followed closely the customs of the old country, a description of the duties devolving upon him will be found interesting. Of course, it could not be expected that the people of the little country village should follow every detail of all elaborate ceremonies, but such was their love of the old home, that they would not relinquish any of their old customs and habits, unless compelled thereto by the force of circumstances.

"On the occasion of a death, the aanspreker was notified, and immediately appeared at the house of mourning. He there received his instructions, and thenceforth assumed complete charge of the whole affair, donning his official dress, which consisted of low shoes, black stockings, black knickerbockers, a black cutaway coat covered by a long, flowing black mantle, a white cravat or bands, and a queer-looking three-cornered hat or *steek*, from one corner of which, to the right, floated a long black crêpe, like a streamer, while on the left corner a rosette had been pinned, showing the sex, and condition (married or single) of the deceased.

"If the latter was very rich or prominent, sometimes ten or twenty aansprekers were employed in announcing his death, and one, usually an old servant of the family, went in the middle of the street, clothed in similar dress, walking along with head bowed, his face buried in a large mourning handkerchief, and led by two aansprekers, one on each side, while the others were making the announcement at the homes. At the time appointed for the funeral, the nearest relations first appeared and partook of some refreshments, generally consisting of a glass of beer or spirits, and smoking a long clay pipe.

"After the arrival of all who were invited, the chief aanspreker ·spoke a few words of consolation, or offered up a prayer, after which the body was carried out on the bier, and was followed in accordance with these directions: 'The relations will please follow, according to rank, the younger members of the family coming first.' All the mourners and bearers were dressed in the same garb as the aansprekers, or else had rosettes pinned to their sleeves, or the lapels of their coats, the aansprekers wearing black or white gloves, according to the sex of the deceased, two of them heading the procession, while the others immediately followed the bearers.

"As the procession wended its way to the cemetery, every one meeting the train stood still uncovered, and stood with bowed head until it had passed. At the grave, the chief aanspreker again spoke a few words, or offered a prayer, and after the burial, led the procession in the same order as before, back to the *sterfhuis*, or house of the deceased. Here beer or spirits, and food, had been prepared for them by the women, who as a rule, did not go to the cemetery. The long clay pipes with tobacco, were on the table, and the mourners ate, drank and smoked, in honor of the deceased. After a short interval, all except the immediate relations departed, and left the bereaved ones alone with their grief."

The requirements of church membership in the early days were positive, sometimes somewhat arbitrary, and discipline strict. Probably on account of the lack of civil courts, many matters considered the proper subjects of legal judicature, were then submitted to the consistory, and consequently, we find them dealing with ordinary crimes as well as with matters that might be considered as pertaining to spirituality.

They were rather intolerant in those days. Methodism and dancing were regarded with equal abhorrence, and subjected to the same punishment, viz., suspension from the church ; while intemperance and other crimes were denounced, and the transgressors subjected to special discipline. In 1790 four regular meetings of the consistory were appointed for each year, and a fine or forfeit of two shillings was exacted from any member absenting himself without a good and reasonable excuse. In 1797, an additional resolution was adopted, which compelled those who did not punctually attend the ordinary meetings, to pay to the consistory the sum of one shilling for every hour elapsed after the time appointed. As the meetings were called for 2 p. m., it was possible to receive considerable income from this source.

Chapter XL.

THE CHURCH.

The church always occupied a prominent place in the consideration of the early settlers, and its services were always regarded as important events in life's experiences, and were well attended. In those days the dominie had almost arbitrary power. On account of his superior learning, his counsel and advice were sought after, and his decision settled all disputed neighborhood matters. It being his duty to instruct and catechise the children, he did so by visiting not only the school, but at intervals, the homes, which were always open to him; and woe betide the unfortunate delinquent, for the dominie's cane was hard, and his right arm strong.

Dr. Taylor says that in 1828 he heard some of his parishioners "speaking of their school days, when they and their mates were busied with their lessons in Dutch and English, using principally the Psalter and New Testament, and rather dreading the day for the good old Dominie's catechise." The sermons were divided into heads with mathematical precision, and each head again subdivided into as many parts as the analytical mind of the old dominie suggested.

The music, no inconsiderable part of the service, at least in volume of sound, was just as vexatious a problem to determine as at the present time. The choir, unlimited as to numbers, grouped about the leader, and pitched their voices to the sound of his tuning fork; and the strains of "Dundee," "China," "Antioch," and "Coronation" echoed and reëchoed, with no uncertain sound. At the suggestion of some unregenerate one, it was decided to add some instrument as an aid to the music. Whereupon a melodeon was procured and surreptitiously placed in the church. So flagrant was the offence, that it was deemed a proper subject for consistorial action; and after proper deliberation, the following resolution was adopted: "Whereas at the instance of some unknown Person or Persons, a Melodeon was placed in the Church without the consent of the Consistory; now, therefore, Be it Resolved, that such Melodeon be allowed to remain."

The communion service was always a specially solemn occasion. A long table, covered with a snow-white cloth, was spread across the end of the church, and around this the communicants in turn seated themselves, to partake of the sacred elements, and listen to the words of encouragement and admonition from their loved pastor.

Up to about 1830, the Reformed Dutch Church at Bergen was the only building used for religious worship in the township, and was resorted to by the worshippers from the outlying farms, from Bergen Point to New Durham; even after the growth of population demanded additional accommodation for church services in other sections, many of the older residents continued their connection with the old congregation, and their attendance upon the services in the old church; and on summer mornings could be seen the sturdy burghers trudging to service, with coat on arm, and smoking the consolatory pipe. As they met, both before and after services, neighborhood matters were talked over, and the results of the season's planting predicted. Questions of Church and State were sometimes so vigorously discussed, especially just before a change of administration, that no little effort was required to curb their earnestness. However, at the tolling of the bell, all wrangling ceased, and with devout mien, they filed into the church, and taking their accustomed places, adjusted themselves in the most comfortable position, ready to receive the spiritual food prepared for their needs.

Chapter XLI.

OTHER CHURCHES.

EPISCOPAL.

CONSIDERABLE space has been devoted to matters connected with the old Dutch church at Bergen, not only because it was the first church organized, but likewise for the reason that under the old order of things it was so closely connected with the civic and social as well as religious conditions then existing. As has been stated, with the growth of the community came demands for other church accommodations, and to meet these, churches were established in rapid succession.

Probably the first church organization in *old* Jersey City was St. Matthew's Protestant Episcopal Society. The first service was held in the upper room of the old Town Hall in 1809 or '10, and on invitation New York clergymen occasionally officiated there. Dr. E. D. Barry afterward became rector, and the worship was continued regularly until the completion of their church building—which is still standing—on Sussex Street near Warren.

The opportunity for the erection of this building came when the Jersey Associates offered a plot of ground 100 feet square, to such religious denominations as would erect a building thereon within a given time. This offer was taken advantage of by the Episcopal, Presbyterian, Catholic and Methodist persuasions, and if the map of Jersey City be examined, it will be seen that a strip of land extending from Sussex to York Streets was donated in accordance with such offer, and is still so occupied by the respective denominations, with the exception of the Presbyterians, whose church passed into the hands of the Dutch Reformed, as related elsewhere.

St. Matthew's Society, having received a bequest of $500, was enabled to commence building, and on the 22d of October, 1831, Dr. Barry laid the corner-stone. Through all the changes that have occurred in lower Jersey City, St. Matthew's still survives, and services are regularly held in the venerable edifice.

Sept. 10, 1851, the Church of the Holy Trinity was organized in old Hudson City, in the school building then standing at St. Paul's and Central Avenues. Gen. E. R. Wright was one of the moving spirits of this enterprise, and associated with him were Thomas Aldridge, Thomas Harrison, David H. Griffith, William Thomas, Jared W. Graves, John Aldridge and James Montgomery. Oct. 8th the first public service was held in the school-house above alluded to, and on Dec. 10th the same year, the corner-stone of the present building was laid by Rt. Rev. Bishop Doane. In July, 1853, the building was duly consecrated, and Rev. W. R. Guis became temporary rector. At the present writing (1902) a modern and substantial edifice is being erected for this congregation on the corner of

Summit and Pavonia Avenues, the present property having been disposed of.

A number of the communicants of Holy Trinity residing in what was known as South Bergen, that is, the region south of Montgomery Street, because of the increase of population in that territory, saw a favorable opportunity for the organization of a new church. Accordingly services were instituted in a small schoolhouse on Gardner Avenue, and in 1860 the congregation was organized as St. Paul's Protestant Episcopal Church. Jno. S. Sutphen and Elizur Ward were elected wardens, and S. D. Harrison, John M. Cornelison, Barberie Throckmorton, Thomas James, Christopher H. Fash, John Rudderow, William P. Bleecker, and Edmund Baldwin, vestrymen.

Rev. F. C. Putnam entered upon his duties as rector, October, 1860. In 1861 a building was erected in Duncan Avenue, followed by the present enlarged and commodious church, which is still occupied by the congregation.

CATHOLIC.

Although there were but few Catholics in old Jersey City at the time of the offer of the Jersey Associates, they determined if possible to secure the advantage of it. After obtaining pledges from the greater number of those residing there, they secured the ground and appealed to their brother Catholics in New York for assistance. Bishop Dubois, at a service held in St. Patrick's Cathedral in that city, urged that assistance be given to the " poor Catholics of Paulus

Hook," and closed his appeal with the following words: " Now all you that will go over there, and aid them to prepare the ground, and help them to begin in the erection of their church, hold up your right hands." Instantly the hand of every male member in the church was raised. The ferry company had promised to convey over without charge all those who would help in the work, and the next day between two and three hundred horses and carts and a large number of men with picks and shovels, wended their way over the ferry, and the filling in of the ground for old St. Peter's (now Aloysius Hall) was enthusiastically begun.

The corner-stone was laid by Bishop Dubois in 1831, but the difficulties encountered were so great that the first mass was not celebrated until 1837. The building was dedicated in 1839, and Rev. William Mahan was the first pastor, followed at short intervals by others until 1844, when Rev. Father Kelly was duly installed as pastor of St. Peter's, and continued as such up to the time of his death, April 28, 1866.

Father Kelly was very closely identified with the early growth of old Jersey City. Quiet and industrious in his habits, modest and unassuming in manner, and yet firm in his adherence to right, and at all times inculcating an honest, upright line of conduct, his name became a household word, and his memory is still fragrant in the minds of those who knew him.

METHODIST.

The Methodist persuasion likewise initiated proceedings to secure their share of the offered gift of the Associates.

At this time the whole territory now known as Bergen and Hudson Counties was included in one circuit, and as was customary, missionary work was done by "circuit riders," faithful men who were ready to endure any privation in order to advance the interests of their faith. The old hymn aptly describes their condition.

> " No foot of land do I possess,
> No cottage in the wilderness;
> A poor wayfaring man,
> I lodge awhile in tents below,
> And gladly wander to and fro,
> Till I my Canaan gain."

A nucleus was gathered, and the property on the south side of York Street adjoining in the rear the plot mentioned above as occupied by the Catholics, was secured. A building was erected in 1835, and Dr. McClintock became the first pastor. Like its neighbor, St. Matthew's, it has withstood all the changes in its neighborhood, and continues regular services at this date.

Elder George Banghart, long a presiding elder of the Philadelphia Conference, was the first to promulgate the doctrines of Methodism in old Hudson City. He is described as a " short, broad-shouldered and deep-chested man, with a loud, clear voice," and was well calculated from a physical standpoint to withstand the persecution and opposition to which he was subjected. He preached at stated times in the old school-house on Bergenwood Avenue, and the first class was formed in 1841, with James Jacobus as leader. The Simpson Methodist Episcopal Church was organized, and meetings continued in this place for three years, when a plot of ground on Cook Street was purchased, and a building erected, which was used until the present building in Central Avenue was finished in 1857. This was then occupied, and still remains the church home of the congregation. The property on Cook Street was sold to the city, and was for some time occupied as a City Hall.

Presbyterian.

In 1809 a Presbyterian Society was formed in old Jersey City, and held services in the Town Hall alternately with the Episcopal congregation for some years. A Presbyterian church was organized Dec. 15, 1825, and in 1828 a frame building was erected on the plot of ground on the south side of Grand Street, allotted to them by the Associates under the terms before mentioned, which was occupied by them until it became the property of the Dutch Reformed Church as already stated.

Presbyterianism appears to have languished in this section for some years, for there seems to have been no movement in this direction until about 1840. April 22, 1844, the "First Presbyterian Church of Jersey City" was organized, and the first services held in the First Reformed Church building above alluded to. Shortly afterward the First Presbyterian Church was erected on the corner of Sussex and Washington

Streets. This building was composed of the identical stone taken from the "stone steepled meeting house" that stood on the north side of Wall Street, New York City. The material of this building was so carefully marked and removed, that, when brought over, it was replaced so that the church was rebuilt on the exact model of, and presented the same appearance as, the original building. The Rev. Jno. Johnston was the first pastor. The old congregation has long since dispersed; many have died, others moved away, and those remaining in the vicinity have united with other churches, the majority of those remaining with the First Presbyterian Church on Emory Street. In 1885 the building was torn down to make room for modern improvements, so that all traces have been obliterated.

In 1855 the need was felt for a Presbyterian church on what is now Jersey City Heights, which, through the energy of John G. Parker and those associated with him, soon crystallized into a movement for the organization of a new society. A number gathered in response to Mr. Parker's invitation, and the first meeting was held in a school building on Storm Avenue. Sept. 16, 1856, Rev. Jas. B. Bonar preached. Oct. 13, 1856, John G. Parker and Orrin H. Crosby applied to the Presbytery of New York for permission to organize a Presbyterian church. Their request was granted, and Oct. 24th the congregation met in the school-house, when twenty-four persons were duly constituted the "First Presbyterian Church of Bergen." Rev. J. G. Craighead, Alexander Bonnell,

Henry Dusenberry, and Orrin H. Crosby, were the incorporators.

Rev. J. G. Craighead, John G. Parker, Jacob M. Merseles, John Raymond, Alexander Bonnell, James C. McBirney, and Elisha Bliss, Jr., constituted the board of trustees, and Messrs. Parker and Crosby were elected elders, and Richard H. Westervelt and Robert D. Wynkoop, deacons.

Edward W. French preached as a supply from Sept. 28, 1856, to Nov. 19, 1856, when he accepted a call as regular pastor and was installed by the Presbytery in the school-house Jan. 15, 1857. Sept. 16, 1857, the corner stone of the building was laid on property acquired on Emory Street east of Bergen Avenue, and Oct. 28, 1858, the church was dedicated.

Owing to the growth of the congregation through the disbandment of the old church in lower Jersey City, and increase of population, the need of greater accommodation was felt, and the building was enlarged; it has recently been redecorated and improved, and is to-day one of the most attractive church buildings in the city.

Chapter XLII.

SCHOOLS.

As has been stated, the education of the young was considered by the early settlers as of equal importance with instruction in and observance of their religious doctrines. Accordingly, in very early times efforts were made to secure suitable instructors.

The first schoolmaster was Engelbert Stuynhuysen, who was licensed October 6, 1662. He was engaged as voorleser, or clerk, with the express stipulation that he, besides this function, was to act as schoolmaster. He was a tailor by trade, and came from Soest, the second city in Westphalia, arriving at New Amsterdam April 25, 1659, in the *Moesman*, Capt. Jacob Jansen. He also represented Bergen in the Landtag, in 1664, and signed the oath of allegiance to Charles II., with other inhabitants of Bergen, on November 22, 1665.

E. Stuynhuysen received a deed of sundry parcels of land in and about the town of Bergen, from Philip Carteret, July 22, 1670. The land comprised seven lots, amounting to about one hundred and fifty acres. So that we may rightly understand what was required of the clerk, it may be well to refer to a resolution passed by consistory in later years. Disputes having arisen concerning the duties of the clerk, it was decided: "He is to perform the services in the congregation both in the church and at funerals, *as has been usual among us.* That is to say, he is to read a chapter in the Holy Bible, the Law, and the Creed, and to sing on the Sabbath, and also when divine service is performed on week days; also, in case of any death in the congregation, he is to deliver the invitations, and shall also provide the gauze at the expense of the consistory, and put it on the chandelier, as soon as the evening service is discontinued every year. (For which he is to be paid fifteen guilders yearly and to charge F4.50 for funeral of each grown person, and proportionately for children.)"

As Stuynhuysen owned his house and lot and double farm, he was required "to act well in his capacity as clerk, not only, but even to look out, and procure himself, a proper and convenient place in which to keep school." To this he objected, and likewise to paying tax of any kind, on the ground that, as schoolmaster and clerk, he was exempt, and that the community should provide a place suitable for such purpose. The matter was submitted to the Schout and Schepens, constituting the government of Bergen, who decreed that he should serve out his contract.

A memorial dated December 17, 1663, was presented to the Governor General and Council at New Netherlands as follows: "Shew reverently, the Sheriff and your Commission of the Village of Bergen, which they presume is known to your Honors, that before the election of the new Commissioners, ye were solicited by Michael Jansen, deceased, to be favored with the appointment of a clerk (voorleser), who should at the same time keep school to instruct the youth, the person of Engelbert Stuynhuysen, who possessed the required abilities, so is, that the Sheriff and Commission now a year past proposed it to the Community; who then approved it, and resolved to engage him, not only as Clerk, but with the express stipulation, that he besides this function, was to keep school, which the aforesaid Stuynhuysen agreed to do, and did so, during five quarters of a year, for which, was allowed him two hundred and fifty florins in seawant annually, besides some other stipulation, the school money so as reason and equity shall demand.

"Now so is, that the aforesaid E. Stuynhuysen, whereas he has a lot and house and a double farm, situated in the jurisdiction of the Village of Bergen, is, by which the aforesaid E. Stuynhuysen considers himself highly aggrieved, and so resigned his office, pretending that a Schoolmaster and Clerk ought to be exempt from all taxes and burthens of the Village, which he says is the common practice through the whole Christian world, which by the Sheriff and Commission, is understood, that only can take place when such clerk, or schoolmaster, does not possess anything else but the school warf, but by no means, when the schoolmaster is in possession of a house and lot and double farm; that he in such a case, should pay nothing from his lot and lands, and the Community at large is of the same opinion, as he receives his salary as Clerk, and not only is obliged to act well in his capacity as Clerk, but even to look out and procure a convenient place to keep school, which he has thus far neglected, and pretends that the Community must effect this, so that he may keep his school in it.

"They cannot perceive how E. Stuynhuysen can be permitted to resign his office, when he neglected to notify his intention one-half year before. Wherefore the supplicants address themselves to your Honors, humbly soliciting them to insinuate to the aforesaid Engelbert Stuynhuysen, to continue in the service the second year, and to declare if the aforesaid Engelbert Stuynhuysen is not obliged by his possession of lot and farm, to provide for the maintenance of a soldier as well as other inhabitants." The petition was granted and Stuynhuysen admonished to continue to the end of his term. As his term of engagement was for two years, it is safe to say that the first school-house was built shortly after its termination, in 1664.

It is evident that Stuynhuysen ceased to act as voorleser about the same time, for the old records of later years state that " B. Van Giesen was buried May 15, 1707, after having filled the office of voorleser at Bergen, for about forty-two years." According to this, Van Giesen entered upon the duties of his office in 1665.

In Carteret's Charter, dated September 22, 1668, is this stipulation : " The Freeholders shall have power to choose their own minister, for the preaching of the Word of God, and being so chosen, all persons as well as the inhabitants, are to contribute according to their estates and for the maintenance, or lay out such a proportion of land, for the minister, *and the keeping of a free school, for the education of youth,* as they shall think fit, which land being once laid out, is not to be alienated, but to remain and continue, from one incumbent to another, free from paying any rent, or any other rate, or taxes whatsoever."

As the population increased, new settlements were formed at inconvenient distances from Bergen, and their people rebelled against paying any taxes for the support of the school, when they were too far away to be benefited. Whereupon "The Schout and Magistrates of the Town of Bergen, requesting that the inhabitants of all the settlements dependent upon them, of what religious persuasion soever they may be, shall be bound to pay their share toward the support of the Precentor and Schoolmaster, and which, being taken into consideration by the Governor and Council, it is ordered, that all the said inhabitants, without any exception, shall, pursuant to the Resolution of the Magistrates of the Town of Bergen, dated December 18, 1672, and subsequent confirmation, pay their share for the support of said Precentor and Schoolmaster." Dated December 24, 1673.

May 24, 1674, the Schouts complaining that some of the inhabitants still obstinately refused to pay quota for the support of the precentor and schoolmaster, the Governor General and Council ordered the Schout to proceed to immediate execution against all unwilling debtors.

Although supported by direct tax, the school was under the direct supervision and control of the church.

The consistory appointed the schoolmaster, who was required, in addition to ordinary instruction in the elementary branches of education, to hear the catechism, and at stated times to receive the pastor and elders of the church, when all the pupils were to be catechised and instructed in the truths of religion; and no person could be appointed to this office, unless he solemnly promised to instruct the children committed to his care in the Principles contained in the Church Standard. It is probable, in the very early days, that the same building served for both church and school, and was likely the one referred to before as having been erected at Tuers Avenue and Vroom Street; but it is well settled that in after years, at least one, or perhaps two, buildings were erected on the present school plot at Bergen Square.

When disputes arose concerning the titles to lands, a commission was appointed to determine the matter, who reported in 1764, that they had regard to the right and allotment due the church and free school, "as in said Charter specified and confirmed, and set off and allotted the sundry lots of land hereinafter described." One of the confirmations and allotments made as stated, was the plot located on Bergen Square where School No. 11 now stands. It would seem from the recent translation of Veerstag, that the second schoolhouse was located on this plot as early as May 11, 1708.

The Records state: "On Tuesday, May 11, 1708, Matheus Bensum has made a beginning with the new schoolhouse, and commenced with the foundation, and

Andrien Vermeulen laid the corner stone;" and the following entry would indicate that many of the citizens of Bergen aided the good work by donating materials:

" Johannis Michielse,	10	loads	stone,
Cornelis Blinkerhof,	10	"	"
Maritje Hartmans,	10	"	"
Johannis Thomasse,	5	"	"
Fredrick Thomasse,	1	"	clay,
Uldrich Brouwer,	4	"	stone,
Johannis Pouwelsie,	8	"	"
" "	3	"	clay,
Matheus De Mott,	1	"	stone,
" " "	10	"	clay,
Jacob Jacobse Van Winkle,	5	"	"
" " " "	5	"	stone,
Robert Seggelse,	1	"	clay,
Jan Lubberse,	5	"	sand,
" "	1	"	clay,
" "	1	"	lime."

This building was probably occupied until the erection of the Columbian Academy, in 1790.

On October 30, 1793, an act was passed called, "An Act for the establishing of Schoolmasters within the Province." Its preamble recites, that "the cultivation of learning and good manners tends greatly to the good and benefit of mankind." The act authorized the inhabitants of each township to meet together and choose three men, whose duty it should be to make a rate for the salary and maintaining of a schoolmaster within the said township, for as long a time as they should think fit ; and it provided that the consent and agreement of the major part of the inhabitants should bind and oblige the remaining part to satisfy and pay their share of said rate, and that the goods and chattels of persons refusing or neglecting to pay were to be distrained and sold. This seems to have been the beginning of the school trustee system, and it may mark the time when the School passed from under the government of the Church.

Chapter XLIII.

COLUMBIAN ACADEMY.

About 1790, by virtue of an act of incorporation, "The Trustees of the Bergen Columbian Academy" took possession of the school lot, and erected thereon the building that in those days attained great prominence. It was a noted institution, and many prominent men of bygone days received instruction within its walls.

An advertisement in a New York paper of August 16, 1796, states: "Agreeably to an advertisement of the 'Trustees of the Bergen Academy,' New Jersey, in April last, the grammar school was opened the first of May, and so continues. The pleasant and healthy situation of the place, its proximity to New York, and the low rate at which board may be had, are advantages meriting the attention of the public, especially the people of New York, who may be assured, that the best care and attention will be given to the education and morals of the children, by the teacher, Elijah Rosegrant. N. B.—The price of boarding, is from twenty to twenty-five shillings per year. The distance of the Academy from Paulus Hook ferry is one and one-half miles only."

Owing to a change of conditions and government, after considerable controversy, "The Trustees of

Columbian Academy conveyed all right, title and interest in the property, to the Freeholders of the Town of Bergen, for the continuance of said free school, and for no other purpose." This was confirmed by the legislature, January 27, 1814, and in after years the property passed under the state school law to the trustees of School No. 1 of the town of Bergen, when the present building was erected. At the time of the consolidation of Jersey City it became a part of the city's school system.

The Columbian Academy was a large, substantial stone building, two stories in height, surmounted by a cupola, on which, after the demolition of the old church in 1841, was placed the weather vane that formerly swung from its lofty spire. The school was conducted on the special grading system, such as is claimed by some of our modern educators as being their own peculiar production, the ground work of which was simply that individuality was recognized, and ability and application encouraged. The whole second story of the building was devoted to educational purposes, with the exception of a square room on the northwest corner, which was occupied by the "Ancient Order of Rechabites," whose mysterious rites kept alive among the scholars a degree of curiosity that was never satisfied.

The initiation services of this order were especially the subject of conjecture; and "riding the goat" being part of the ceremony, a great desire was manifested to see this notorious animal. Holes were bored through the door during the daytime, in order to get a peep at

COLUMBIAN ACADEMY.

the uncanny beast; but beyond a faint rustling, no evidence was ever secured. He was said to be of the razor-backed, high-stepping variety, and it was supposed that the victim suffered untold tortures during the ceremony.

This room changed the form of the school-room from an oblong into an L-shape, a fact that was taken advantage of by the discreet schoolmaster, to place the girls at one extremity and the boys at the other, with his desk in the angle, so as to afford him general supervision over all. This arrangement was convenient for the punishment of any refractory or disobedient pupil, who was placed between two of the opposite sex, there to remain until the fault had been sufficiently atoned for; this proceeding was always resented by the boys, but when the process was reversed, it was received by the girls with a due amount of commendable resignation. It is curious to note how often it became necessary to subject them to this punishment.

As there were no janitors in those days, the semi-weekly cleaning and sweeping of the school-room was performed by two of the larger girls, who were selected for this purpose by the schoolmaster, as a mark of special favor; and one boy was detailed to assist them by carrying water, etc., as a matter of punishment. Under the circumstances, a long time was required to perform this work, and oftentimes the shades of evening were falling before it was satisfactorily completed. On one occasion, the schoolmaster, passing the building about nightfall, noticed an open window, whereupon he determined upon an investigation. He discovered that the sweeping had been finished some hours before, but that the girls had invented a new game which required the most active exertion on the part of the boy to escape being kissed. It is related that the boy was in this instance found in such an exhausted condition, that this department of co-education was forthwith discontinued.

The school-room was furnished with a large stove, which in cold weather was kept red-hot, thus presenting an attractive surface at which to project pieces of rubber, assafœtida or other substances producing pleasant perfumes when burned. In case of extreme cold, the scholars were allowed to surround this stove by details; after one section was well warmed, at least on one side, it was followed by another, somewhat after the manner of relieving guard in a military camp, and as the process continued in an endless succession, the danger of any scholar being frozen to death was avoided.

Long benches without backs were provided for the smaller pupils, while desks with three compartments were furnished for the more advanced scholars. This division of the desk was taken advantage of by the occupants, who fitted a lock on the middle one, ostensibly for the purpose of protecting the luncheons of those who lived at a distance, but principally for hiding contraband articles and forbidden sweets.

Underneath the corner room alluded to was a similar one, in which, according to the fitness of things, a shoemaker located himself, so as to be convenient for covering balls, furnishing whip lashes, or supplying the penny's worth of strap oil, for which the innocent youngster was sent. At a convenient distance, opposite the old parsonage, that stood at the northwest corner of the square, was a large weeping willow, well calculated to hide those naughty boys who, attaching a string to the clapper of the old school bell, concealed themselves within its friendly branches, so that they might, unseen, ring the bell at unseemly hours, and startle the staid inhabitants from their slumbers.

On account of the size of the Columbian Academy and the difficulty of organizing a regular faculty with one head, there were often two distinct schools under its roof. On one occasion, Gasherie DeWitt had charge of the school on the upper floor, while one Gahagen was installed on the lower floor. These were both individual enterprises, independent of each other, with separate and distinct charges for tuition. The rate most frequently charged was $1.50 per quarter. As may be imagined, considerable competition existed between the schools, and when necessary to influence pupils, concessions from the above amount were made. The income of the principals depending upon the number of pupils they might secure, they were very active in their canvassing, and at times rivalled the arts of the practised politician to accomplish their aims. The usual school year in the early days was divided into four quarters of twelve weeks each, with two weeks' holiday in both spring and fall. This was intended to allow proper time and opportunity for replenishing the summer and winter wardrobe.

Chapter XLIV.

OTHER EARLY SCHOOL ACCOMMODATIONS.

IN the course of time, increased school facilities were demanded, and private enterprises instituted several small schools in different sections of the town, which met with varying success. One was held in the early days, in the old parsonage that stood on the site of the present Bergen Reformed Church. Another school was opened by Sylvester Van Buren in the Van Riper homestead, which stood west of Bergen Avenue and south of Montgomery Street. He taught the boys, while the instruction of the girls came under the direct supervision of his wife and daughter.

John Welsh and his son James shortly after started a school in a small building, formerly used as a carpenter shop, that stood near the corner of Bergen and Harrison Avenues. This increased in numbers to such an extent that a long, low, one-story building was erected on Harrison Avenue west of what is now Monticello, for its accommodation. After his father's death, James Welsh became sole proprietor. His method of instruction was to a great extent of the muscular sort, and he controlled and disciplined his little flock through their fears. He was of a somewhat nervous, irritable temperament, and was oftentimes so unjust in the treatment of his scholars that open rebellion was frequent, in several cases resulting in their withdrawal from the school. Frequently the parents of the rebels, recognizing the justice of their active protests, sustained them, and either allowed them to finish their education at home, or sent them elsewhere for that purpose. Notwithstanding this severity and lack of discretion in school government, however, Schoolmaster Welsh was well versed in the requirements of the age, and there are those still living who recognize that the foundations of their intellectual acquirements were firmly planted by him.

This building in later years was followed by another, which was erected on the corner of Harrison and Monticello Avenues. This was afterward enlarged, and under the present municipal government is known in the school system of Jersey City as School No. 16.

The first school building for upper or North Bergen section, was in the territory of old Hudson City. It was a small, one-story frame structure, located about the corner of Bergenwood and Beacon Avenues, and was the forerunner of School No. 6. During the continuance of the school in this building, a financial report was read, which ignored a balance of six cents remaining on hand at the end of the previous fiscal year; whereupon an explanation was demanded, and it was found that at the meeting at which such previous report was submitted, after the report had been prepared, it was discovered that artificial light would be needed, and that amount was expended for tallow dips. At this time, the teachers were obliged to depend upon whatever could be collected from the scholars, which was supposed to amount to an annual contribution of about $2 per pupil, although this was by no means certain.

For lower Jersey City, the first school was started in a building located on Sussex Street, in the rear of the present U. S. Post Office. It was erected in 1809 on ground donated by the Jersey Associates, and was used as a town hall, lock-up and school. Several years after, the first public school, sustained by subscription, was held in this same building, and soon became quite flourishing, in evidence of which fact we have the following extract from the message of Mayor Peter Martin in April, 1840: "A Public School has been established on such liberal principles that any resident of the City, however poor he may be, may avail himself of its benefits. The highest price for tuition per quarter, demanded of any pupil, is $1.00—the lowest 50c., but children whose Parents or Guardians are not able to pay for their tuition are not on that account debarred from the privileges of the school. It is in a flourishing condition, nearly 300 pupils having availed themselves of its benefits the past year."

July 23, 1843, an ordinance was adopted by the Council of Jersey City, which recites: "That all monies that may hereafter be received from tavern licenses, the city quota of the surplus revenue, the interest of the city proportion of the Bergen Corporation fund, be, and the same are hereby appropriated, to the support of Public School No. 1, kept in the

Town Hall, and such other Public Schools as the Common Council may from time to time erect and establish." The school was to be open quarterly, under the direction of the township school committee, and the general supervision of the Mayor and Common Council. The pupils were to reside in Jersey City, and pay fifty cents per quarter for spelling and reading, or one dollar when writing, arithmetic and other branches were included. This school was continued until 1847, and was under the charge of Albert T. Smith. February 8, of that year, Mr. Smith became the principal of the first public free school in Jersey City, with Geo. H. Linsley as first assistant. This building was located on the site now occupied by Public School No. 1.

GEO. H. LINSLEY.

In 1851 Mr. Smith resigned, and Mr. Linsley succeeded him as principal, which position he has held continuously to the present time. Mr. Linsley is a born teacher and a close student of human nature. He inspires the love and confidence of his pupils to a remarkable degree through his sympathetic nature and conscientious performance of the duties pertaining to his position. Recognizing the individuality of every pupil, he implants within each one the desire for better and higher things, and teaches them that without self-exertion no success .can be achieved. It was the exercise of these qualities that made him the successful instructor of over half a century, loved and revered by the whole community.

From these small beginnings in different parts of the territory, our present magnificent school system has grown and developed.

Other individual educational enterprises were instituted, and had much to do with moulding and influencing the sentiment and policy of the whole community. In 1839 Wm. L. Dickinson, who became so favorably known in the educational world, opened the Lyceum School on Grand Street, and continued there for many years. He afterward became a member of the School Board, and was elected City and County Superintendent. As such, by his wise and judicious action, he inaugurated many reforms and gave a decided impetus to the work of education.

WM. L. DICKINSON.

Messrs. Dickinson and Linsley were near neighbors, and possessing similar tastes and congenial dispositions, they became close and sincere friends. They counselled and coöperated in all matters pertaining to educational advancement, and to them was due the early organization and development of our school system.

Other notable instances were "The Misses Graves' Seminary for Young Ladies," located at the corner of Summit Avenue and Cottage Street, adjoining the present Baptist Church; "The Miss Chadeayne's Seminary," at the corner of Green and Grand Streets; and "Hasbrouck Institute," founded as a preparatory collegiate institute for boys. Of these notable institutions, only "Hasbrouck Institute" survives. It was founded by Doctor Washington Hasbrouck in 1856, and the school then occupied a small building on Mercer Street, near Wayne. Dr. Hasbrouck conducted this school for ten years, and many of its graduates are now occupying positions of prominence and responsibility in the city. It has since then greatly developed, and is recognized in educational circles as an institution second to none in its facilities for and methods of instruction.

It is curious to note in an examination of the old records, how frequently lotteries were resorted to as a means of obtaining funds for many enterprises. The moneys needed for the support of educational institutions, and even for the repairing and building of churches and parsonages, were procured in this way. The advertisements in the daily prints of 1759 to 1773 give abundant evidence of the universal practice of this method of obtaining funds.

Chapter XLV.

THE GROWTH AND CHANGES OF "OLD BERGEN."

PERHAPS no more fitting introduction to this division of our subject can be found than the address delivered by Chief Justice Hornblower on the occasion of the dedication of the new court-house in March, 1845, as published in the *Jersey City Advertiser* of that date. He said:—

"I remember the old town of Bergen, when it had very few inhabitants except old-fashioned Dutchmen, and very few houses, except those not built for show, but for domestic comfort and convenience; long, low, and unpretending in appearance, but durable in materials, and opening upon the street some two or three hospitable doors, into which the friend and stranger might enter and find a welcome, and from which they might retire, and leave a blessing behind them. Hoboken then consisted of little besides a well kept public house, and a beautiful retreat from the noise and bustle of the neighboring metropolis" (The Elysian Fields).

"No Jersey City then adorned your shores, nothing but a large, long ferry-house, occupied successively by an Ellsworth, a Smith, and a Hunt, with here and there a boatman's or a fisherman's cabin, that stood upon the heap of sand called Powles Hook; your settlements were scarce, your occupations agricultural and industrial, and your population small but healthy, peaceful and honest. You needed, for many years within my recollection, but one physician to administer to your physical necessities, and but one man of God to supply your spiritual want, and not even one lawyer, to satisfy your litigious propensities, for you had none to be satisfied. Peace reigned throughout your borders. Simplicity of life and manners, and honesty of purpose, were the prevailing characteristics of the good old Dutch, who almost exclusively occupied the soil of your county, in the days of my boyhood. A court at Hackensack, and a few Dutch justices at home, were all you wanted to punish the few offenders, and settle the few lawsuits that troubled you in those days. But alas! we fear those good old days have gone by, never to return. The rapidly increasing population of our county, the vast improvements in science and the arts, and the enterprising spirit of the age in which we live, have wrought a mighty change, even within the period of my memory. The facilities of steamboats and railroad cars, and the increasing spirit of trade, and commerce, and manufacture of the arts, have brought the good old town of Bergen into contact with the world, cut up her territory into small localities, studded her shores with splendid buildings, turned her farms into country seats, her cabbage grounds into pleasure gardens, and her dwelling places into workshops and manufactories. Such, in fact, has been the change in appearance and population, of that part of the old County of Bergen, that I can scarcely retrace the steps of my boyhood, when in my visits to my friends here or in the City of New York, I used to traverse these hills."

The changes alluded to in this interesting discourse of the venerable Chief Justice have continued with redoubled speed, and in an increasing ratio, and the great city, which has consolidated much of the ancient territory and absorbed the numerous small municipalities, is without doubt, destined to rival the greater New York, by gathering in all of the contiguous territory, and perhaps reaching out to and including the green hills of Orange.

The early inhabitants of Bergen were strongly imbued with the peculiar characteristics of the Fatherland, and for years clung with a persistent tenacity to the habits and customs they had brought with them. Rescued from the silt and sand of the ocean, the people of the Fatherland were endowed with a love of country and attachment for the home that were but intensified by the successive struggles and privations to which they were subjected, and they transmitted to their descendants, an intense perseverance, frugal thrift and untiring industry—qualities of no uncertain value in the settlement and development of a new country, and which have made them prominent, not only in the commercial and mercantile world, but also in civil and military life.

Until about the year 1840, or thereabouts, the township of Bergen did not change much in the character or habits of its population. Possessed of the old

Dutch characteristic of holding on to the paternal acres, inherited from their fathers, they would undergo extreme privations rather than voluntarily part with their patrimony so that it was almost an impossibility to secure from the original owners a plot of ground even of sufficient size on which to build a house.

In the course of time, however, owing to the passing away of the original owners, and the resultant necessary division of the home acres, or the financial embarrassment of some unfortunates, the territory was gradually opened up to the investment of outside capital. The increasing population of New York City created a demand for convenient homes, and Bergen, from its proximity and healthful surroundings, received much attention. Attracted by its quiet neighborhood, its primitive surroundings, and its pure sparkling water drawn with the old-fashioned well sweep and moss-covered bucket from rock-embedded springs, there were many who frequented this spot. A few succeeded in securing temporary board, and being thus brought into contact with the inhabitants, dispelled the existing prejudice against strangers. Many of these, in course of time, secured plots of ground, which they improved and beautified. As it was but occasionally that such plots were thrown on the market, there could be no concerted or uniform action in relation to the improvements, but as opportunity offered, these plots were laid out and built upon, to suit the tastes of the owners.

Had there been, during the early development of the

territory, an opportunity for such united action, Bergen Hill would have been noted as the most attractive suburb of the commercial and financial center of the world. Commanding as it does views of unsurpassed beauty, its atmosphere purified and tempered by the invigorating ocean breezes from the east, or the fresh, pure air direct from the Blue Mountains on the west, with perfect drainage facilities, and of easy access to the neighboring city, it promised to become the choice spot for the ideal home.

The tenacity with which the old settlers held on to what they determined were their rights was marked. But though unwilling to concede to an unjust demand, they yet recognized the rights of others, and were always willing to effect an adjustment of any difficulties—from their own individual standpoint. Good-natured yet decided, controversies were indulged in, sometimes being only definitely adjusted by due course of law. It is related that two of the old neighbors, becoming involved in some differences, appealed to the old Dutch justice for an adjudication. The session occurred on one of the hot days of late summer, and the court was instituted under the shade of an overhanging apple tree. The legal talent of the day was engaged, and indulged in lofty flights of eloquence, stimulated thereto by copious cooling drinks of applejack. After a thorough consideration, the matter was determined in favor of one of the litigants, and a moderate amount of money adjudged to be due to him; whereupon the whole sum was placed in the hands of the justice, and he was instructed to expend the same in an old-fashioned jollification, in which all the interested parties, witnesses and spectators were invited to join. The narrator neglects to supply the final closing of the case. As the popularity of the old justice from this time rapidly increased, it may be safely assumed that he held the scales with an even hand.

Chapter XLVI.

GROWTH AND CHANGES CONTINUED.

ALTHOUGH the Village of Bergen was prescribed within certain boundaries, as heretofore mentioned, the name attached itself to its outlying plantations and dependencies; and as it was the seat of justice and the location of the courts, the surrounding territory for a considerable extent was designated by the same name. Consequently when the province was divided into counties in 1682, it was but natural that the name of Bergen should attach itself to that portion of the territory including this venerable town.

As the development and prosperity of the state continued, it was found advisable to make smaller political divisions, and in 1709 an Act was passed setting off the County of Bergen as follows: "That on the Eastern division the County shall begin at Constable Hook, and so run up along the Bay and Hudson River, to the partition point between New Jersey and New York, and along that division line to the division line between the East and West sections of the Province, to Pequannock River, thence by such River and the Passaic, to the Sound, and thence by the Sound to Constable Hook where it began."

The rapidly changing conditions, with increase of population, necessitated political alterations, and old

Bergen County, in 1837, was subdivided, the present Passaic Country being taken therefrom; and in 1840, the County of Hudson, with its present metes and bounds, was set off, leaving the remaining territory existing under the old name of Bergen County. Hudson County contains the old village of Bergen, and the Bergen Township, practically identical with the old Indian Grant of 1658.

In order that an accurate idea of the growth and transformation of this territory may be obtained, we will follow closely, yet briefly, the different changes that have occurred.

C. Van Vorst was the owner of a large tract of land at Paulus Hook, having obtained patent for same March 31, 1663, located between Harsimus and Jan de Lacher's Point. This property was located south of the present Newark Avenue, and extended to Communipaw Cove, reaching to above Merseles Street.

The Duke's Farm, north of this, extending from Newark Avenue to Harsimus Cove, was owned by one Kennedy. He was envious of the exclusive privileges enjoyed by Van Vorst for operating the ferry to New York, and endeavored to secure the same for himself. After considerable controversy, Van Vorst was eventually successful, and such rights became vested in him.

April 14, 1804, Van Vorst sold part of the above property, including ferry privileges, to Abraham Varick, merchant. He transferred same to Anthony Dey and others, who afterward formed " Associates of the

"OLD BERGEN."

Jersey Company," who thereupon became invested with the title of the property. At this time the ferry was moved to a point between Grand and York, and near the center of the block on which Colgate's factory now stands. At this time the horse-boats elsewhere described were used, but these were displaced by steamboats in 1812. Says the *Sentinel of*

OLD FERRY.

Freedom: "The first trip drew thousands of spectators to both shores, attracted by the novel and pleasing scene. One may now cross the river at the slight cost of fifty cents, same as on bridge."

Up to 1852 the rates of ferriage from Jersey City to New York were fixed by the Board of Chosen Freeholders of Hudson County, and it is curious to note how the amount charged was based upon the article carried. Appended are some of the rates fixed by the Board in Sept., 1849.

Every person on foot above ten years old,	.03
Every person on foot under ten years and above five,	.02
Man and horse only,	.09
Ordinary 4 wheeled truck loaded, 2 horses,	.37½
Ordinary 4 wheeled truck light, 2 horses,	.25
Coach, coachee, chariot, phaeton, etc.,	.30
Wagon load of hay or straw,	.50
Oats, green peas and beans, per bushel,	.01
Potatoes, per bushel,	.01½
Barrels containing apples or vegetables,	.06¼
Oysters, per bushel,	.03
Fancy chairs, each,	.02
Common chairs, each,	.01
Sofas and pianos, each,	.25
Bureaus,	.12½

An additional sum of 3 cents each to be charged every person on any vehicle in addition to the driver, who is included in the first charge.

The first evidence of the disintegration of the old township of Bergen was in 1820, when the City of Jersey was incorporated (re-incorporated in 1829 as Jersey City). It comprised that part of the territory, bounded between the present line of Grove Street, on the west, and the Hudson River on the east, with the Bay as the southerly boundary line, and reaching north to Harsimus Cove, being part of the property alluded to above, as having been owned by Van Vorst. It contained at that time about three hundred inhabitants. Gordon's *Gazetteer* states in 1834: "Jersey

City is commodiously laid out in lots twenty-five feet by one hundred, distributed into forty-five blocks, each two acres, with broad streets, and contains many good buildings." Van Vorst Township was taken from Bergen in 1841, bounded north by North Bergen, east by Hudson River and Jersey City, south by New York Bay, and west by Bergen and North Bergen.

North Bergen was formed in 1842, and comprised all the territory of old Bergen Township lying north of the New Jersey Railroad, and between Van Vorst Township and Hackensack River. Secaucus is a strip of land lying in the western part of this township, and surrounded by marshes.

Hudson City was erected in 1855 from the territory of North Bergen, and was the southerly portion thereof, bounded directly by the New Jersey Railroad, and extending north to the line of the Paterson Plank Road. It had been previously separated from Bergen, in 1852, and was first called the Town of Hudson.

In this territory likewise, numerous little settlements sprang up, each possessing its own characteristics, and each known by its distinctive name, such as Washington Village, West Hoboken, North Hoboken, Union Hill, Guttenberg, Weehawken and New Durham, all telling of rapid growth.

To the southward, the Township of Greenville was incorporated in 1863, and at that date was cut off from the Township of Bergen, and was bounded on the north by Linden Avenue, reaching down to the Morris Canal. From its commanding and healthful situation, it was early sought as a place of residence, but the love of the early settlers for their acres, and their consequent unwillingness to part with them, for some time retarded its growth. Owing, however, to the passing away of the original owners, and necessary division of the home acres, as has been said, much has been thrown on the market, since which time the town's growth has been constant and rapid, until to-day it has become a most important part of Jersey City, into which it became incorporated at the time of consolidation in 1872.

At Communipaw, Lafayette was laid out. It had no direct connection with Jersey City, on account of the impassable nature of the marsh that surrounded it, until a foot path was built by driving sharpened stakes into the soft meadow ground, and placing planks over them. This means of communication was often entirely interrupted by high tides, which frequently carried away the precarious foot path. The extending and filling in of Pacific Avenue, to and connecting with Grand Street, made a direct and reliable connection, and caused the rapid growth of that vicinity.

Bayonne was incorporated in 1869, and comprises all the southern portion of the peninsula lying between the New York and Newark Bays, south of Morris Canal.

Hoboken, now become a city of considerable magnitude, was purchased by John Stevens in 1804, as previously stated, who shortly after had the same surveyed and laid out into building lots; and many were sold. In 1838 Stevens formed the Hoboken Land and Improvement Company, which was incorporated on February 21, of that year. He transferred much of the land to this Company the following year, and a uniform system of improvement was instituted, the wisdom of which policy has been emphasized by the rapid growth and the attractive character of the improvements. Hoboken was set off from North Bergen in 1849, and incorporated as a city, March 28, 1855.

Bergen, after having been dismembered to form other municipalities, was incorporated as the Town of Bergen in 1855, its area comprising but little more than the old town as originally surveyed, and the out-gardens in its immediate neighborhood. March 11, 1868, the City of Bergen was incorporated and Henry Fitch elected first Mayor. In 1872 it, with other towns, was absorbed by, and became part of, the City of Jersey City. Like many of its old families, it has lost its name and identity, but its influence continues, even to the present time, in the shaping and directing of the general municipal policy. All of the above mentioned territory (outside of the Town of Bergen) was originally attached to the old town. It comprised the "*buytentuyn*," or out-gardens, of its inhabitants, and at the close of the Revolution was very sparsely settled. The growth of the neighboring city of New York caused a demand for near-by homes, and from time to time, settlements were made, until at the present time, the whole territory is occupied by a thriving population.

Chapter XLVII.

CHARACTERISTICS OF THE INHABITANTS OF "OLD BERGEN."

WASHINGTON IRVING has somewhat satirically and in an amusing manner ascribed to the early Dutch settlers many habits and peculiarities, which, while not strictly accurate and historical, were suggested by the fact that the early Dutch were so tenacious of the habits and customs descending to them from their forefathers, and so indifferent to the affairs and wrangles of the outside world, that even in those slow-going days, their conservativeness and opposition to all new and untried theories, were particularly noticeable. Although under the shadow of the great city, and within easy access to it, they disregarded its activities and pursued their avocations, undisturbed by its allurements. If they did not indulge in its extravagances or possess its luxuries, they were contented to enjoy their home comfort, with no desire to adopt any of the wild or unusual habits introduced by the royalists, of which they doubtless often heard.

The fertile soil of "Old Bergen" afforded ample recompense to the old Dutch husbandman, and he cared for his acres with a judgment and industry that returned him a most liberal remuneration. Throughout this section, cabbage was the principal staple of produce, and immense quantities were raised, not only for supplying the neighboring city, but for shipment to all parts of the country; and even as late as during our Civil War, from its beginning in 1861—when the shutting off of Southern transportation cut off the early supply from those parts—to its close, the market gardens of this territory furnished a goodly supply of this succulent vegetable, and the successors of the original settlers reaped an abundant reward. Another source of income to the early farmers, in addition to the vegetables, grain and hay, raised and sold, was the cutting and bunching of clover, which in its green state was readily sold to the denizens of New York as a most healthful and necessary food for their horses and cattle.

In the fall, the marshes on either side of the hill were frequented by hunters in search of the wild-fowl that congregated there, and oftentimes great flocks of wild pigeons, settling in the woods on the west side, afforded sport and sustenance, not only for the residents, but for many who crossed over from the neighboring city.

Many of the inhabitants, especially those living at Communipau and in the neighborhood of the shore, derived a most comfortable living, and oftentimes a competency, from the oyster and shad fisheries of New York and Newark Bays. From the time that Hudson regaled himself on what he termed the largest and most luscious bivalves that were ever seen, until very recent times, when the increase of manufactures, and consequent befouling of the waters destroyed the beds, these oysters enjoyed a most flattering reputation.

The spinning and weaving of wool and flax occupied the women of the day. Their industry was able to furnish the necessary clothing for daily comfort, and frequently with provident forethought, the housewife prepared for every emergency. The well stored *caas* or clothespress was furnished with the finery deemed necessary to envelope the form of the comely bride; and from it the beautifully crimped and plaited garments were brought forth for the enshrouding of the dead.

The frugal mode of life of these people, and their economical habits, were rarely departed from, and resulted in an accumulation which was prudently invested and increased. As tillers of the soil, they seemed to become imbued with the healthfulness, as well with the strict honesty and integrity, of Dame Nature, learning well, not only that without honest exertion no adequate and regular return could be expected, but also that with a proper application and cultivation—dealing justly with her—they would be assured of a bountiful reward.

During the occupation of New York by the British army, the settlers of "Old Bergen," as they bartered with the invaders for their farm produce or garden truck, secured most valuable information, by means of which Washington was oftentimes enabled to thwart the enemy's plans. The first news of the intended treachery of Benedict Arnold, was conveyed to

Washington through one of the sturdy patriots of Bergen Hill, it having been learned by one of the female members of his family, while marketing in New York.

The names of the early settlers were selected on account of some special characteristic, their trade or calling, or the place of their birth. Thus we find Gerit Gerritse (that is, Garret the son of Garret) as having received a patent for land at Bergen, from Philip Carteret, May 12, 1668. He came from the city of Wagening, an ancient town near the Rhine; and *van* signifying *from* or *of*, he was designated as Garret Van Wagening, which became the family name. So the name of Van Buskirk is composed of two Dutch words *bos*, woods, and *kerch*, church; hence with the Van, the name signifies " from the woods by the church." Jacobse Wallings in the early days came from Middleburgh, the capital of Zealand, and as he was a storekeeper, was called Jacob Van Winkle, *winkle* signifying *store* or *shop*, hence " Jacob of the shop." The custom of retaining family names made it often very difficult to designate the different members of the same family with the same patronymic, and so in time they were localized; as in the Van Horne family, various members were known as John, Johns John, Trinches John, Mill Creek John, Canal Bridge John, etc.

One custom which made it almost impossible to trace genealogies was that of giving a child as a surname his father's christian name with *se* or *sen* (meaning *son*) added. Thus if a child was baptized Hendrick and his father's name was William, he would be known as Hendrick Williamsen; if his son was called Jan, he would became Jan Hendricksen. If his son was called Garret, he would be known as Garret Jansen; and the next generation might become John Garretson; the next, Michael Johnson, and so on indefinitely. So that, as will be readily seen, identical names would frequently occur in families entirely separate and distinct. The inconvenience of this practice and the confusion it occasioned, caused its abandonment, and the names borne by the heads of families at this time became and continued the family names.

Chapter XLVIII.

THE WARS OF 1812 AND 1861, AND OLD LANDMARKS.

AFTER a period of peace, there were again rumors of trouble with Great Britain, and her insistance on the " Right of Search " made another outbreak probable. The bitterness engendered during the Revolution was revived, and once more the territory of Bergen was aroused by the bugle call and the martial tread of armed hosts. War was declared, and active measures were adopted for the defence of New York City, which was supposed to be the objective point of the enemy. New York State being threatened at her northern border, and most of her troops being employed in that direction, she was obliged to rely on New Jersey for the protection of her chief city. August 13, 1814, Gov. Pennington of New Jersey issued his proclamation for the enrollment of men, and ordered a force, composed of different companies of the state, to march immediately to Paulus Hook, where Brig. Gen. Colfax was to assume command.

Some of these troops were encamped at and surrounding the " Old Arsenal," that stood on the north side of Summit Avenue, about midway between Newark and Hoboken Avenues. Gen. Swift reported to Gov. Tompkins of New York, that the Jersey troops were enrolled and occupied a fortified camp at

Bergen Heights. They consisted of twenty-three companies, and as soon as inspected, were formed into regiments, under command of Col. J. W. Frelinghuysen. Some were stationed at Paulus Hook, and some at Sandy Hook, while those remaining encamped at Jersey City Heights were kept in readiness, in case of any attempted entrance into the Bay or attack upon New York.

They were never called upon for active service, however, as during that campaign, active hostilities were carried on upon the Canadian border and in the neighborhood of Washington. The treaty of peace was signed December 14, 1814, but before that date, it was apparent that the end of hostilities was drawing near, and the need of a defensive corps removed. On December 1, 1814, this brigade of New Jersey militia was paid by the Corporation of the City of New York, and discharged from the service of protecting that city. Col. Frelinghuysen wrote to Gov. Tompkins December 9, 1814, expressing great satisfaction at the treatment of his troops by New York, and stated they would be in readiness at all times to act in her defence. On returning to their places of rendezvous, the war being ended, the militia were mustered out; and the war clouds having disappeared, the people again settled down to their avocations.

But once more, in the days of '61, the fires of patriotism blazed brightly, as the boom of the gun fired on Sumter proclaimed the beginning of an unnatural strife. It is hard at this distance of time and under prevailing conditions, to thoroughly appreciate the intensity of feeling that prevailed during those troublous days. No foreign foe threatened our shores, but internal dissensions clouded the future with doubt and uncertainty ; ties of blood and interest were rudely torn asunder, and neighbor looked askance at neighbor, while men spoke with bated breath. There were white faces and troubled hearts, but the patriotic citizens of " Old Bergen " showed no signs of faltering, and when the call for troops was made, they were among the first to volunteer for the defence of the national capital.

April 15th, 1861, Simon Cameron, then Secretary of War of the United States, wired Governor Olden of New Jersey that he had just sent a despatch, calling on him for four regiments of troops for immediate service. The governor, without waiting for the receipt of the official paper, which by the way was not received until the 17th, at once communicated with all sections of the state. On the following day, April 16th, a meeting was held in the City Hall, Jersey City, for the purpose of aiding in the enlistment of troops ; and volunteers being called for, immediate response was made.

On the Sunday following, patriotic sermons were preached in all the churches, which raised the feelings of the people to a white heat. The figure of old Dr. Taylor is vividly recalled, as with quivering lip and streaming eyes, he implored that the red hand of war might still be stayed, but pointed out in most emphatic terms the great danger of apathy and the necessity of instant preparation, so that the purpose of those who would pull down the whole fabric of our government might be thwarted. At his invitation, Company A of the 2nd Regiment, Capt. Garret D. Van Reypen, largely recruited from within the confines of "Old Bergen," marched to the church on the following day, to receive at his hands a testament for each member, together with his blessing and God-speed.

On the 22nd, a committee of five citizens was appointed to provide for the equipment and transportation of the regiment, which duty was so promptly performed that on the 26th, only four days after, and ten days from the first notification, the 2nd New Jersey Regiment was encamped at Trenton, prepared to enter upon an active campaign. This was the more notable, as the North was at the time completely unprepared for war. The necessary expense attending the sudden call for troops was borne by individuals, who were afterward reimbursed through the issue of local bonds. This War Committee was continued throughout the war, and took under their special charge the families of those who were thus suddenly called away. Large amounts of money were subscribed, by means of which, under its judicious management, the general government was relieved of much embarrassment.

The thrilling accounts of these troublous years may be found in detail in our state records, and the names of those honored heroes emblazoned upon her escutcheon.

In the old days the ridge of high ground extended in an unbroken front, save for the indentations of natural ravines or water courses, from Greenville north ward, until it merged into the grand old Palisades, the wonder and admiration of the world. Following from its commencement an almost direct line to about the present line of Academy Street, it there jutted out in a bold promontory, from eighty to one hundred feet high, called "Point of Rocks," where the Pennsylvania Railroad round-house now stands, and then receding, followed about the original line northward. The stream of water known as Mill Creek flowed in from the Bay just north of the high point of land, now levelled, near the present junction of Jersey Avenue and Phillip Street, and in a curving line through the marsh until it reached the Point of Rocks; thence it followed the base of the hill northward to near Hoboken Avenue, where it mingled its waters with a stream that flowed into Harsimus Cove. This creek was of considerable importance both for commercial reasons, and as a means of communication with Bergen Town.

The farmers loaded periaguas at Newark Avenue (where the West Shore freight house now stands) with garden truck for the New York market; and in the early spring, when escaping frost rendered the road from Communipaw well nigh impassable, the devout worshippers at that place, loath to lose the privileges of the sanctuary, took boat to Point of Rocks, and there clambered over the rocks at Academy Street, or followed the steep ascent of Mill Road, and thence through the lane opening on Bergen Avenue at Foye Place, to the church.

With the exception of a few farm clearings, until a comparatively recent day the whole of the northerly part of the township was covered with dense woods, which likewise continued in an almost unbroken line along the western slope all the way to Bergen Point. There were also extensive groves at intervals along the eastern brow of the hill, notably at Weehawken

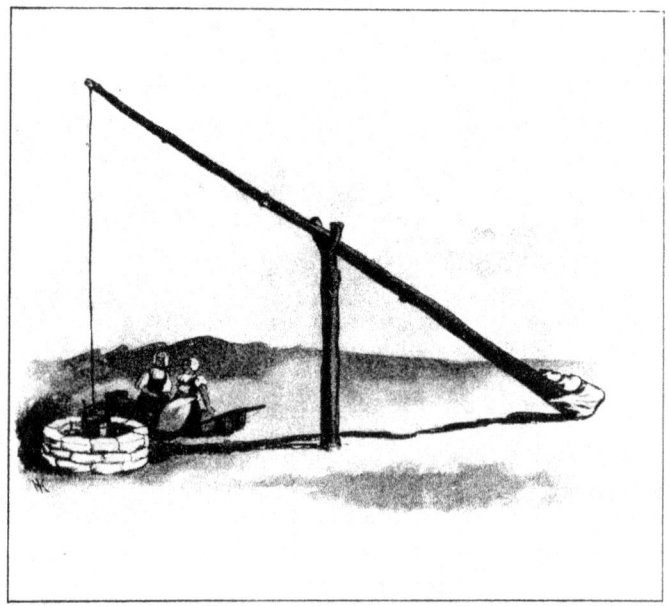

"OLD WELL."

and North Hudson. As has been mentioned, one of the great attractions of "Old Bergen" was its sparkling spring water. The purity of this water was greatly appreciated, and numberless wells were sunk throughout the territory. They were walled up with stone, and during the early days, like the old well in the Square, were surmounted by a well-sweep with bucket. So cool were they that they were utilized during the hot months for the preservation of butter and meats, which were lowered to within a few inches from the surface of the water, and there kept suspended until needed for use.

In 1850 the population, especially of lower Jersey City, had increased to such an extent, that the water supply from the old wells not only became inadequate, but many of them were abandoned on sanitary grounds, and covered over. During this time, drinking water from the wells on the Heights was carted around and sold by the pailful. Public attention was thus directed to the necessity of procuring a new and full supply. In 1851 a water company was incorporated, and about three years afterward, the water service and reservoirs were completed. The source of supply was the upper part of the Passaic River, which at that time afforded a generous supply of good potable water.

June 30th, 1854, the reservoirs were filled and the water let into the distributing pipes. An event of such great importance was marked by a special celebration, in which the whole community joined. A procession was formed of leading citizens, escorted by fire and military companies, many of these from neighboring cities, which wended its way from lower Jersey City, though the principal streets, and to and around the reservoir at Central Avenue on the Heights. The long line of blue and red shirted firemen, drawing their well polished and gaily decked machines and encircling the reservoir, was indeed an inspiriting sight. The rejoicings were general, and the day was concluded with banquets and congratulations.

Some of the old wells, however, continued in use to within very recent years. Many a thirsty wayfarer has had reason to bless the old Academy Street well that was located for centuries on the north side of that street about midway between Tuers and Summit Avenues. And even at the present day, pilgrimages are made by many to the old well still in use on the Van Riper homestead, corner of Academy and Van Reypen Streets, from which has continued to flow the clear, refreshing water since the very foundation of the town.

In the early days conflagrations were infrequent, and when they did occur they brought out all in the vicinity, with pails, pans or any vessel suitable for holding water. These were passed from hand to hand by establishing long lines, from the nearest wells or cisterns to the fire. As buildings became more dense, some new method was demanded and volunteer companies were formed. These were maintained at first by subscription—but afterward became a city charge, with no pay attached for service. Those were palmy days, and the rivalry between the different companies resulted in prompt and efficient service. No old fireman can recall without a thrill, the being roused at midnight by the clang of the fire-bell, and almost unconsciously donning the clothing which was always conveniently placed, and then rushing, plunging, jumping, rolling down the stairs, and landing in some mysterious way, yet scarcely awake, in the fire boots that stood at the foot. Then intent on gaining the post of honor (the tiller) in advance of any other, he would speed to the engine house and strain every nerve to move the machine toward the scene of conflagration. The excitement would grow apace, as the different companies struggled in their endeavor to "get on first water," and the hoarse shouts of the firemen and the clanging of the engine pumps excited an enthusiasm that seems to linger through all the passing years.

There are still standing some of the old dwellings, erected far back in colonial times, which bear evidence of the substantial manner in which the houses of those days were built. The Demotte and Zabriskie mansions at North Bergen, the Van Horne homestead at Communipaw, the Gautier home at Greenville and the Vreeland house at Cavan Point are instances; and could the walls of these venerable structures speak, many tales of the privations and sufferings of the early settlers, as well as much secret history of the Revolution, would be rescued from the oblivion into which they have fallen. The Gautier home was originally built by one Tom Brown in 1760, who was a privateer, and in 1747 married a Van Buskirk, who had inherited a large tract of land, on a part of which the building stood, it being contained in the patent confirmed by Governor Carteret in 1667 to Lawrence Adriense.

This Captain Brown was the person who established and maintained a ferry across the Hackensack, known as Brown's Ferry, which after 1715, when the road to Newark was laid out, was one of the connecting links in the stage route from New York to Philadelphia. He was a sturdy patriot, and espoused the cause of Independence with great vigor. Tradition states that in his early days he became very familiar with the coast of Africa, and frequently ran into the harbor a cargo of slaves, some of whom were confined in the cellar of the house, while he was negotiating their sale. The old home was likewise the scene of many gatherings, attracted thither by the well-known lavish hospitality of its owner; and its spacious banqueting hall and roomy parlors entertained many of the notables of the day in feasting and revelling, such as was peculiar to the early times. During the Revolution it became the rendezvous for patriot officers and sympathizers, whose drooping spirits were often inspired through the genial hospitality so bountifully dispensed within its walls.

The Vreeland homestead was another ancient building that stood a few hundred feet north of the one just mentioned, being located like it on the shore of the Bay. It was a conspicuous object to all sailing up the harbor, and its prominence subjected it to rather rough usage. During the early colonial days and the Revolutionary War the old house sustained many attacks from the Indians, and many a bullet hole in the old oaken wood-work testified to the fierceness of attack and defence. During the Revolution, an English war ship opened fire upon the house, and in after years a cannon ball, imbedded in its wall, was shown as proof of the danger to which its inmates were subjected. In this, as well as in its neighbor before spoken of, many a merry dance was held and countless guests royally entertained by the old Dutch settlers.

The absorption of the valuable water-front of Communipaw by our large railroad corporations, and the consequent filling in and docking out, have forced the "old settlers" away, and one by one they have departed, some to that other country where rest and peace continuously prevail, while the later generations have moved to more pleasant surroundings, until at the present writing but one remains (Mr. Garret Bush), who, amid the changes and encroachments, still clings to the home of his fathers. The charm that lingered so long over the old settlement has gone, and the ancient roof-trees have been demolished or so changed that the spirit of "Long Ago" has fled, never to return.

The following newspaper clipping of 1873 is of interest as showing how, even to that late date, the old hamlet slept in pristine quietude. "The ancient hamlet of Communipau, lying on the New Jersey shore within sight of New York, is a precious relic of the days long gone. Two centuries and a half have hallowed its fields and homes as the dwelling places of men. Only a cannon-shot distance from the Battery, it sleeps across the Bay in its ancient Dutch repose, only a half hour from the marble and gilt of the new, to the moss-grown homesteads of the old; only a half hour from the dash and rattle of Broadway to the whispering of the thousand shells that yet line the quiet beach of old Pavonia."

There is a tradition that one day in early spring there appeared two strangers upon the shore of Communipaw, who, seeking out the "oldest inhabitants," strove to gather such traditions and reminiscences as they were able. The one was very talkative and entertaining, while the other wandered about at will and gathered up much of the material which, woven into the delightful fabric with which Diedrich Knickerbocker has enveloped the early history of our Dutch ancestors, has endowed it with such resistless charm and attractiveness.

In the translation of an account of a voyage to New Amsterdam in 1679 we find the following, which shows somewhat of the settlement and surroundings. Says the traveller: "Intending to visit Communipau, our landlady told us of another good woman who lived at that place named Fitje, and recommended us to visit her, which we did as soon as we landed. We found her a little pious after the manner of the country, and you could discover that there was something of the Lord in her, but very much covered up and defiled. We dined there and spoke to her of what we deemed necessary for her condition. She has many grand children, all of whom are not unjust. We continued our journey along a fine, broad wagon-road to the other village called Bergen, a good half hour or three-quarters inland from there."

Chapter XLIX.

CHANGES AND OLD LANDMARKS CONTINUED.

UNTIL very recently at Communipaw, on the high, projecting bank near the Old Mill Creek, hard by the site of the Indian massacre of the early days, stood the Van Horne farm-house. From its prominent position, affording a full view of the waters of the bay and surroundings, this house became a favorite "look-out" for the Americans during the Revolution, and a system of signals was agreed upon to be given from this point, as a warning to those of the settlers who had ventured across the bay to sell their produce to the British army, whenever any danger was to be apprehended from the Tories or refugees lurking in the neighborhood. It was the habit of the enemy to lay in wait for the returning burghers and rob them of the proceeds of their sales.

Northwest from the Van Horne house was the Race Track, established in 1769 by Cornelius Van Vorst. It was laid out on the sand hills, then standing between York Street and Wayne, and above Varick. It was one mile in length, and was a noted place of resort for the lovers of sport from New York and the surrounding country, until the Revolutionary War. After peace was declared, it was again opened, but was discontinued in 1808, when a new track was established at Harsimus, near the Erie Railroad at Henderson Street.

Near the corner of Green and Montgomery Streets, (at that time the river bank), at a point now occupied by the Pennsylvania Railroad tracks, Isaac Edge in 1815 built a windmill, which was taken down in 1839 and removed to Long Island. In 1856 Lewis A. Edwards of Orient, Long Island, wrote in relation to it: "Your old windmill though 'demolished' is not 'defunct.' It was placed on board of vessels and conveyed around the eastern extremity of the North Branch of Long Island into Town Harbor, and from thence taken to Mill Hill in the town of Southold, in Suffolk County, where it was again placed upon its pins, as natural as life.

EDGE'S WINDMILL.

"We live in a migratory age, but a migratory windmill, even at this day, may be considered a novelty. The old mill is now in an excellent state of preservation, notwithstanding its forty years' wear and tear, and one h u n d r e d and twenty-five miles of travel, and I venture to say would stand as severe a tilt with 'Don Quixote' as any mill I ever came in contact with."

A short distance south of the Old Mill, between

York and Grand Streets, and about one hundred feet east of Green, was the ferry landing, alluded to elsewhere. April 1st, 1839, this was moved to the corner of Hudson and Montgomery Streets, and at the time of the extension of Exchange Place, was changed to its present location.

The ferry facilities at first consisted of a gallows frame, painted green, supporting iron pulleys, over which a chain was passed, one end of which was attached to the floating bridge, while to the other end balancing weights were fastened, so that the bridge could accommodate itself to the rise and fall of the tides, thus facilitating the loading or unloading of the boats.

The row boats, and periaguas or sail boats of the early days were succeeded by what was called the horse boat on the Paulus Hook ferry. In this the propelling power was obtained by means of an endless moving platform, after the manner of a tread mill, on which a horse walked, and which turned a paddle wheel by a combination of cog-wheels. Sometimes slaves were employed for this purpose, and the weird songs in which they frequently indulged greatly relieved the weariness of the passage.

The first steamboats used on this ferry were composed of two hulls fastened strongly together, leaving a space between, in which was suspended a paddle wheel. One side of the boat, over one hull, was intended for the accommodation of vehicles and cattle, and the other side was furnished with seats for passengers. Both sides were uncovered, but below the passenger side, a cabin was fitted up, so that in case of stormy or inclement weather, the passengers might seek protection from the elements. There were two of these boats, named respectively *York* and *Jersey*.

Early one Sunday morning in February, 1816, during a season of extreme cold, there were seen on an ice floe floating in the middle of the river, two men seemingly engaged in fighting. One would knock over the other, and, taking him sometimes by the hands, and again by the heels, drag him over the ice some distance; then standing him up, would knock him over, repeating the process continually. The affair created great excitement, and finally a row boat with four men put off to ascertain the cause of the strange conduct. Reaching the floe, they discovered the men to be the U. S. Mail Carrier and his negro, who had left Paulus Hook the previous evening, but were caught in the floating ice. They had rowed up and down seeking for a passage through to the New York shore, but were unsuccessful. Feeling the effects of the extreme cold, they determined to take to the ice, and by vigorous exercise, escape being frozen to death. The poor negro, succumbing to the intense cold, wished for nothing but to be allowed to sleep. The carrier, knowing that this would prove fatal, adopted the drastic treatment that had fortunately attracted attention, and in doing so, not only saved the negro's life, but probably his own, by indulging in this violent exercise. The negro was found by his rescuers with nose, ears and fingers frozen, and they were obliged to lift him into the boat and carry him to shore.

At this time the Southern Mail consisted of two bags, carried over to New York by row boat.

In the early days the mail communication of the people of Bergen with the outside world was very limited, and what few letters there were, were brought from the offices at Newark or New York by any one who visited those places, and distributed as occasion offered, being sometimes handed round at the church door on Sunday and sometimes left at the general store until called for. In 1807, General Granger established an office in a store in lower Jersey City, at the corner of York and Washington Streets, from whence the mail was distributed at first in the old way, or else by carriers, who collected the postage and delivery, the amount charged depending upon the distance of the place from which the letter was sent. Some time afterwards a sub-station was established at the Five Corners, where mail bags from the Jersey City station were left by the stages in passing. The mail for the town of Bergen was called for with considerable regularity by the school boys, who left any letters for the neighborhood at the store on Bergen Square.

An interesting story is told in connection with the mail distribution of the day. General Cummings was for many years one of the stage proprietors, and also contractor for carrying the mail. Many irregularities occurring in the delivery of the mails, the then postmaster, Gideon Granger, determined to personally investigate the cause, and travel over the mail routes in disguise. General Cummings, being informed of his inten-

PRIOR'S MILL.

tion by a friend, gave certain instructions to his negro driver, in case he should have a passenger answering a certain description.

A short time after, as the stage was about starting from Paulus Hook, the driver detected a suspicious-looking personage entering the stage, whereupon, gathering up the reins, he started his horses off at a tremendous pace over the corduroy road, between Newark and Paulus Hook. The occupants were violently jostled about to the great danger of life and limb. Gideon called out to drive slower. "Cawnt do it, massa. I drives the United States Mail," answered the driver, as he urged the horses to still greater speed. Granger begged him again and again to slacken his speed, but was met with the unfailing response, "Cawnt do it, massa. I drives the United States Mail." On the arrival of the coach at Newark, it is said, Granger was so bruised that he showed no disposition to continue his investigations, being satisfied that at least one contract was being faithfully carried out.

Prior's Mill was built during the early colonial days and was located on the Old Mill Creek, heretofore described, near the present crossing of the Junction R. R. with Railroad Avenue. It was what was known as a tide-water mill, and was operated by the force of the outflowing water upon the wheel. A dam was built across the creek, with gates arranged so as to admit the incoming tides, but which closed as soon as the pressure against them ceased. The imprisoned water was then led by a sluice-way against the paddles or buckets of the water-wheel, causing it to revolve with sufficient force to turn the mill stones by which the grain was ground.

The bolt as it was called, separating the chaff from the flour, was operated by means of an iron winch, which was turned by the slaves, giving forth first the flour, then the middlings, and lastly the bran. As the mill could be operated only on the ebbing tide, the times for grinding were very irregular, there being as it were two sessions every twenty-four hours, and these varying with the tides. The clanking of the mill wheel and the rumbling of the stones, accompanied by the darkies' songs, were calculated at nights, when the mill was dimly lighted with the flickering blaze of a tallow lantern, to send those indescribable thrills along the spine that most of us have at some time experienced.

The prominent places of resort for the sporting element of the day, were the Beacon Race Course and the Thatched Cottage Garden. The former was located just north of Hoboken Avenue, between Palisade and Summit. Here several noted races were run, and attracted many of the sporting men of New York, as well as those of the surrounding country. But after a short season of activity, like its successor at Guttenberg, it succumbed to the unhealthful influences of the neighborhood.

The Thatched Cottage Garden, located at Essex Street, in lower Jersey City, was the scene of many athletic games and balloon ascensions. In this connection, it may be well to mention an episode that at the time attracted much attention. One Gillie, an

THE THATCHED COTTAGE. *Front and rear view.*

aeronaut, was in the habit of making ascensions with a captive balloon, and descending by means of a parachute. Among those who witnessed this feat was a resident of "Old Bergen," who, in his desire to convey the idea to the minds of a crowd of admiring youngsters, gave what might be called an object lesson. Procuring a rope and clothes basket, they wended their way to a large barn, one rainy Saturday, and throwing the rope over a beam near the rafters, fastened one end of it to the basket, in which the would-be aeronaut seated himself, with an umbrella in his possession. Instructing the boys to hoist him up to the beam, and to cut the rope at his word, he soon reached the elevated position. Then raising the umbrella, he gave the word of command; but alas for his confiding nature, the force of gravitation proved too strong for his frail support, and he descended to the floor with such force, that he was laid up for some time, with fractured limbs. This may have been the origin of the saying, once so much used in this vicinity for cautioning against any act of folly, "Don't be a Gillie."

At Newark and Summit Avenues stood the official hay-scales, which, although not constructed on the lines observed in our delicately balanced modern machines, was nevertheless a decided improvement over the method used in Indian times, before alluded to. A stout crane was suspended in the center, from one end of which depended four heavy chains terminating in rings, which were slipped over the wheel hubs of the hay wagon. From the other end was hung a platform, on which were placed fifty six pound weights, sufficient to balance the load.

Chapter L.

CHANGES.

But time has wrought many changes, not only in manners and customs, but in the whole topography of the country. Hills that were long sacred to the sports of childhood, are now levelled, and the many ponds over whose glassy surface steel-shod feet glided for many years, have been filled up so that not a trace remains. Tuers Pond, located along the line of Water Avenue, was in the winter, by a little judicious management, made to overflow the surrounding fields, producing a magnificent expanse for skating.

By a comparison with present conditions some idea may be formed of the changes that have occurred along the whole shore line, of the old township of Bergen. From Weehawken on the north to Constable Hook on the south, not only have the coves and bays that formerly indented the coast been filled and utilized for manufacturing and commercial purposes ; but they have been encroached on to such an extent that thousands of acres have been added to the growth of the lowlands, which through natural causes accumulated at the base of the rocky heights, against whose walls, through passing years, the waters of the Bay dashed, as driven by the strong east wind, or gently murmured, as the ripples broke upon the shore.

"OLD BERGEN."

The spots from whence the Indian launched his canoe, and the shores first trodden by the feet of the early traders, are now hidden forever beneath the accumulation of filling that has placed them thousands of feet inland. At Communipaw, the only spot where the shore has been left on its original line until the present, operations have been initiated which will in a short time completely obliterate the original ferry landing place of colonial days. Here almost a mile to the eastward may be seen the outward bulkhead line that marks the limit to territorial expansion.

Just north of the Pennsylvania Railroad cut, east of Baldwin Avenue, one of the giant monarchs of the forest was standing as late as 1860. This point was resorted to by many lovers of nature, on account of the unsurpassed view presented from that spot. Being of unusual prominence, it commanded an exceptional view of the whole Bay, with its surroundings. On the one hand, could be seen the distant gateway to the ocean, guarded by the wooded heights of Long and Staten Islands, while Governors, Bedloes, and Ellis Islands, like emeralds in a silver setting, added to the beauty of the scene. Around this spot, and in the neighborhood of the old tree, Lafayette with his command encamped on August 24, 1780, and although in full view of the enemy, conducted from thence successful raids through Bergen and Bergen Neck. To the northward, Castle Point jutted out, standing like a sentinel watching the approach to the Highlands.

Feb. 24, 1820, an act was passed by the state legislature which gave freedom to every child born of slave parents subsequent to July 4, 1804, males at twenty-five, and females at twenty-one years of age. The inhabitants of "Old Bergen," however, had been for some years gradually freeing the slaves left to them under the old conditions; on the death of an old resident, it was generally found that he provided in his will for the manumission and at least partial support of his dusky retainers. But notwithstanding this fact, many of the old house-servants refused to avail themselves of the privilege, and continued as voluntary dependants until their death. Provision was made, however, for their descendants, and through the liberality of their old employers quite a settlement was formed along the Old Mill Road between Academy and Montgomery Streets. Many of these were for a time distinguished by the prefix of the family name of their old owners before their own, and they emphasized their approval of this custom by fully expecting, and in some cases demanding, support, when through their natural improvidence they had failed to make provision for "a rainy day." Some time in the Fifties a church was erected for their exclusive use on the line of the Old Mill Road south of Academy Street, and for many years was the scene of energetic and enthusiastic services.

A little farther south, or between what is now Mercer Street and Fairmount Avenue, east of Summit, and extending over the brow of the hill to the edge of the marsh below (now Cornelison Avenue) was a dense woods of pine and cedar, in the recesses of which, during the existence of slavery, runaways were accustomed to hide. They were here provided with food by their fellows; or if, by reason of extra watchfulness on the part of their masters, this source of supply was cut off, they issued forth in the darkness of the night to procure food or other plunder. When these depredations became too frequent or especially flagrant, a regular hunt was organized, and the outlaws captured and subjected to punishment, which was sometimes very severe.

In these woods, near where the City Hospital now stands, was a spot made sacred to the negroes as the shrine about which to gather on "Bobilation Day," the anniversary of the abolition of slavery throughout the state. Near this, on the spot now enclosed between Church and Montgomery Streets and east of Summit Avenue, was Newkirk's pond, a resort of the more exclusive, which being surrounded by a cedar grove, was sheltered from the wintry blasts. The overflow from these ponds passed down through the low ground on the line of Monticello Avenue, to about where it is now intersected by Gardner; thence diagonally across Crescent Avenue and Park Street, to a point near the Junction, fell over a ledge of rocks called the "offall," crossed Communipaw Avenue, and emptied its waters in a creek on the meadows back of Communipaw, and afterwards into the Morris Canal.

On the rocks at the head of Academy Street, near the site of the old fort, was a favorite picnic ground; and although the way over the rocks was steep and precipitous, daring riders forced their horses over a

THE OLD TAVERN.

The Old Tavern near the Church also alluded to on page 178, still standing on corner of Bergen and Glenwood Avenues, built in part of the material of the old Stuyvesant Tavern of Colonial days which stood in the same spot. In the rear wall may be seen the old corner stone with the letters P. S. cut in.

path leading into Railroad Avenue. But there is a consecrated spot on Bergen Avenue south of the Square, to which our memories often turn; for old "Aunt Rachel's" ranch afforded club privileges equal to the best equipped of the present day, and within its friendly shelter plans were laid and plots concocted, without any danger of interference by the outside world.

At the corner of Glenwood Street and Bergen Avenue stood an old tavern, built in the early colonial days, which was a favorite stopping place for refreshments with Washington and his officers, while their escort encamped in the Tuers orchard opposite, on part of which the Fourth Regiment Armory stands. This old hostelry was justly celebrated for its cooking, and its fame continued to a very late day. Even down to the Fifties, when, after the fatigues of the Annual Training Day, the officers were constrained to seek refreshment with which to regale themselves, this noted place was selected with a unanimity that betokened previous favorable acquaintance with its cuisine.

At Bergen Square on the southeast corner still stands the old De Mott homestead, modernized of course, where Gen. Washington enjoyed the lavish hospitality of its owner. On the east side of Bergen Square just south of Academy Street, a whipping post stood, and such was the terror inspired by the severe flagellations inflicted by the town constable, that wrong doers kept aloof, with the result that the community enjoyed an unusual sense of security. In fact, fifty years ago no locks were used on the doors, and frequently throughout the hot summer nights, the upper halves of the doors were left open, so as to afford free ventilation. Sometimes the roystering spirits of the day took advantage of the confidence exhibited by the "Old Settlers," and the good dame found in the morning that some of her luscious pies and other goodies had vanished during the night. But this, being only an occasional occurrence, was submitted to with resignation and regarded as but the result of youthful exuberance.

Sometimes, however, the improvident blacks, unable to withstand the temptation to which they were subjected, purloined the pork and corned beef that were carefully "laid away" in the cellar for the winter's use. This seems to have been regarded as an unpardonable sin, for a general search was made, and the offender was made to realize the truth of the admonition that "the way of the transgressor is hard." When captured, he was taken to the whipping post, and, his outer clothing having been removed, was made to clasp his arms about it; his feet were then fastened at the ground and, his wrists being tied together, his arms were drawn up and fastened by means of a rope passing through the top of the post, and the punishment inflicted.

The constable then in a loud voice told of the nature of the offence and descanted upon its enormity, counselling repentance and a return to the way of uprightness, pronouncing sentence of banishment in the meanwhile. The last two persons punished in this way were two men who were detected in the act of thieving, a colored man and his dissolute white companion.

A short distance from the Square, on the west, fronting on the opposite sides of Academy Street, are the Van Wagenen and Van Reypen homesteads. To the north, about two hundred feet from the Square on Bergen Avenue, is the Sip homestead, and near by, on the opposite side, the Hornblower house, the site of Capt. Forsyth's outpost during the Revolution, before mentioned.

A burying-ground for the colored people was located in Van Reypen's orchard, between the Boulevard and Van Reypen Street, about two hundred feet southerly of a line projected west from the south side of Academy Street. There was also one about the center of the plot bounded by Bergen Avenue, Enos Place and Newkirk Street. This was formerly an Indian burying-ground, and in recent years, when an excavation was made, human bones were found that indicated the interment of a race far above the average height.

The last interment in this spot was Newkirk's Sam, as late as 1853. He had been during the latter part of his life engaged specially in the care of a team of horses belonging to his employer, which were in the nomenclature of the day called, "Dick horse" and "Sal horse." Sam always entertained a warm affection for Dick; and when in the course of time, the horse succumbed to the feebleness of old age and died, Sam earnestly besought his employer to bury the horse in this old burying-ground, so that he himself could be buried along side of him, exacting a promise to that effect. It is needless to say that this promise was adhered to, and Sam's last resting place was by the side of his faithful old friend, for whom he had an abiding affection. Sam, by his integrity and faithfulness, had won the respect of many of the neighbors, and his funeral services from the old Newkirk homestead were largely attended by both black and white.

In his earnestness in the dissemination of some of his doctrines, Sam sometimes neglected to gauge his capacity for the spiritual consolation in which he indulged, with the result that on one occasion at least, he was so overcome that he was placed in a chair and borne to his home by the hands of sympathizing comrades. Some time after, on being shown the picture of an Indian prince carried in a sedan chair, he recalled his experience, and ever afterward boasted of his princely method of locomotion, claiming it as an evidence of his royal descent.

On an eminence on the bank of the Pennsylvania Railroad cut, near the east side of the Boulevard, can be still seen the Tonnelle homestead, the scene of much merry making in the olden time. The estate extended to Summit Avenue, and from Pavonia Avenue to near the present line of the Railroad. The house is substantially built of the enduring granite of Bergen Hill, and with a little renovation may be made to last another century. The approach to this house was from Summit Avenue, and was rather imposing. Heavy iron gates suspended from massive stone pillars guarded the entrance, while on either side of the well shaded lane were grassy enclosures, well stocked with deer, while the shrill cry of gaudy, bedizened peacocks greeted the welcome visitor.

At the Five Corners were sundry hostelrys convenient for the refreshment of the weary traveller, even from colonial days; and in later years these were resorted to by the socially inclined who wished to indulge in the periodical gatherings for the " D.D.'s," —dancing and dinners—and were likewise selected as the most convenient place for the voters of " Old Bergen " township to exercise their right of franchise.

From " Lee's Memoirs " we learn that Washington's favorite position was near " the western shore of the Hudson, which was always considered by him the point of connection of the two extremes of the Union." He frequently met his generals on the hills of " Old Bergen," and there discussed the projects on the execution of which the fate of the young republic depended. And it is well authenticated that, on one occasion at least, he and Lafayette dined together under an apple tree that stood in the orchard of the old parsonage, on the northwest corner of Bergen Square.

From a letter descriptive of the visit of Lafayette to this country in 1824, I quote: " On his arrival at Jersey City, remaining but a short time, the General, with His Excellency, Governor Williamson, entered a superb carriage drawn by four beautiful bay horses, and a cavalcade was formed, which proceeded leisurely toward Newark. Arrived at Bergen, it was found that the inhabitants of the little town had assembled at the tavern, on the southwest corner of Summit and

Newark Avenues, and were so anxious to pay their respects to the General, that he was constrained to alight for a moment.

"Here unexpectedly, he was addressed by a delegation from the Town, and presented with a cane made from an apple tree, under which, when passing through that town during the Revolution, he and Washington dined. The cane is richly mounted with gold and bears the following inscription on the top: 'Lafayette,' and around the head, 'Shaded the Hero and his friend Washington in 1779. Presented by the Corporation of Bergen, 1824.' As the General re-entered his carriage and left this ancient town, he was heartily cheered."

At the breaking out of the war of 1812, the United States government secured a plot of ground on the west side of Palisade Avenue, between Hoboken and Newark Avenues, where an arsenal was erected. This was likewise used as a barracks for enlisted men during the Civil War. Opposite the arsenal was the Harrison estate, by which name the property is still known. It is located on the brow of the hill east of Summit and between Newark and Hoboken Avenues. It was noted for the lavish hospitality and sporting proclivities of its owners, some of whom met an untimely end by their indulgence in their favorite pastime.

Chapter LI.

HOBOKEN.

At Hoboken was the " Elysian Fields," the fashionable pleasure resort of the day, and crowds daily wended their way thither from New York to enjoy its shady walks and quaff the refreshing beer dispensed in this vicinity. It was here that P. T. Barnum instituted a buffalo hunt in the Forties. He chartered all the boats plying to Hoboken on the day appointed, and by judicious advertising, of which art he was a past master, attracted a great crowd to see the sport. Unfortunately for the seekers after excitement, the sedative qualities of Hoboken's atmosphere produced such an effect on the " wild untamable " animals, that they refused utterly to be disturbed in their meditations, and the only real hunt that took place at the time was that for sufficient refreshment with which to regale the famished multitude.

This was likewise the scene of many hotly contested athletic games, and many barbecues were held here. It was in short the spot where all lovers of sport in those days were wont to congregate. Along the river bank, under the shade of Castle Point, was the Sibyl's Cave, where cool, refreshing water that bubbled from the spring located there, was sold to thirsty wayfarers at one cent a glass.

Of early Hoboken, Lawrence La Bree thus enthusiastically writes : " There was no lovelier spot dotting the bosom of the Mahakenaghtus than the little island known as Hoboken, or by the Indians called Hobuk. Its shores on either side were laved by the waters of the great river, and the beauty of its scenery made it one of the favorite haunts of the red man. Its most prominent point overlooks the waters of the bay, and commands an extensive view for some distance up the river, the entire scope of the island, and the cliffs and mountains to the westward and northwest. Here met the savages in council, and here arose their conical huts ; here were chanted their war songs, and here each season were celebrated the festivities of the harvest feast. Here the swart chief, the leader of a thousand braves, recounted his victories, and exhibited the trophies of an hundred battles, and the young warrior stretching his lithe limbs upon the green sward, beneath the branches of the overshadowing oak, wooed the nut-brown maid and charmed her soul with his passionate declarations. Beautiful island, like an emerald set in the bosom of an Indian princess, there was no peer above thee in all the bright waters around that kissed thy shores as amorously, as ever the fondest lover breathed his adoration on the lips of his mistress. No foe could approach them unobserved, for watchful eyes scanned continually the surrounding waters. The fame of the braves had reached the great tribes of the west, and secured for them immunity from the raids and attacks of wandering bands."

As before stated, Nicholas Verlett received a grant of Hoboken from Gov. Stuyvesant in 1663. His granddaughter married one Robert Hickman, who sold the land, June 9, 1711, to Samuel Bayard. The latter erected a country residence at Castle Point, where he was wont to retire to escape the summer heats, and entertain his friends and acquaintances in the princely manner for which he was noted. Bayard was an enthusiastic royalist, and joined the English army at the beginning of the Revolutionary troubles. During the war his property was raided several times, and on August 24, 1780, his residence was burned by a foraging party of Patriots, who obtained considerable plunder, and carried off a number of cattle. Under the Act of 1778, this property was afterwards confiscated, and it was sold by the government to John Stevens on February 7, 1787, whose descendants still retain the ownership of a considerable portion of the territory.

To the energy, liberality and wise policy of the Stevens family, much of the present attractiveness and prosperity of Hoboken is due. Mr. Stevens, who was closely identified with the early history of Hoboken, was an engineer of wide reputation, as well as a natural practical machinist. He was far in advance of the times, and often promulgated his theories at the risk of ridicule and contumely; he was continually engaged in experiments tending toward the improvement and betterment of the human race, and was pointed at as one of those enthusiasts who had gone daft because of close investigation and study. When the Legislature of New York was considering the construction of the Erie Canal, "Col. Stevens of Hoboken astonished that body by announcing that he could build a railroad at a much less cost than the proposed canal, and on which the transportation by means of cars drawn by a steam locomotive could be carried at a much cheaper rate and at a much higher rate of speed than was possible on any canal."

He was laughed at and called a maniac, and some of his best friends thought he had lost his mental equipoise through experimental science. Even Chancellor Livingston, in a letter dated Mar. 2, 1811, says: " I had before read of your very ingenious proposition as to railroad communication. I fear, however, on mature reflection that they will be liable to serious objections. . . . In case of necessary stops or stays to take wood or water many accidents would happen. . . . Upon the whole, I fear the expense would be much greater than that of canals, without being so convenient." Present results have proven the truth and wisdom of Col. Stevens' assertion.

The City was regularly laid out in 1804, but for some reason it did not commend itself as a place of residence for some years. In 1834 it was described as a place "built chiefly on one street. It contains about one hundred dwellings, three licensed taverns, and many unlicensed ones, four or five stores, and between six and seven hundred inhabitants. It is remarkable chiefly, however, as a place of resort for the citizens of New York during the hot days of summer. The bank of the river is high, and the invigorating sea breeze may be enjoyed at almost all hours when the sun is above the horizon.

"In the walks along the river bank, over the grounds, and in the beautiful fields studded with clumps of trees and variegated by shady woods, the business man of New York finds a momentary relaxation and enjoyment in the 'Elysian Fields,' and the gastronome, whether of the Corporation of New Amstel, or an invited guest, may find a less rural, but not a more sensual pleasure in the feast of Turtle."

Another description worthy of note because of its truthfulness is as follows: "On Sunday afternoon we stepped into a small steamboat bound across the river, where lie in all their natural and cultivated beauty the 'Elysian Fields,' meant to be, I suppose, a second edition of the Heaven of the Ancients, but judging from a description of the one, and the sight of the other, the modern scene is neither greatly improved nor enlarged. There are many hills and dales, winding walks, grass-covered plains, and shaded seats in great profusion, and altogether they do much credit to the taste of the proprietor and the public. There appears to be a considerable degree of levity amongst those who resort to this spot of Sunday recreation, which is but little in accordance with our Scotch notion of Presbyterian propriety."

Rev. Dr. Abeel, who was stationed at English Neighborhood in charge of the Reformed Dutch Church at that place between 1825 and 1828, sometimes visited the territory of Hoboken and adjacent thereto. Finding at Hoboken several of the residents identified with the Reformed Dutch Church, who were wont to cross the river to New York to attend religious services, while others were connected with the congregations at Bergen, he urged upon them the advisability of establishing a church there. Hoboken at this time was sparsely settled, it being mainly considered a place of recreation and enjoyment for the pleasure-loving denizens of New York. On Sundays especially, multitudes thronged its borders, and the whole day was devoted to all manner of pastimes. There seemed no opportunity for the holding of public worship, but Dr. Abeel finally arranged with one of the hotel proprietors for the occupancy of his ball-room on Sunday evenings, for the purpose of worship. It was not deemed judicious to attempt services until after the crowds had departed, and accordingly the time of assembling was to be determined by the ringing of the last ferry bell. The boats left Hoboken for their last trip at eight o'clock, and it was the custom to ring the ferry bell vigorously·at that hour so that the belated traveller would hasten his steps. Consequently it was full half an hour later before the services commenced.

These services were held intermittingly until 1828, when Dr. Abeel was succeeded at English Neighborhood by Rev. Philip Duryea, and he, in connection with Rev. Dr. Taylor, of Bergen, alternated the Sabbath evening services twice in each month. These services were held in the old schoolhouse, and continued until about 1830, when the Protestant Episcopal

Church was erected through the liberality and coöperation of several families belonging to that denomination. On account of the then existing conditions, it was not possible to sustain more than one religious enterprise, and the Dutch Reformed services were discontinued, several of the congregation worshipping at Bergen and New Durham. With occasional attempts, no permanent result was secured until Sept., 1850, when an application was presented to the Classis for establishing a Reformed Dutch Church. This request was granted and the church organized Oct. 27th the same year.

Hoboken was likewise noted as the home of the "Hoboken Turtle Club," that coterie of Epicureans, who rivalled the old Romans in the variety and abundance of the feasts they prepared.

Chapter LII.

HOBOKEN AND TRADITION

TRADITION relates a sorrowful romance in connection with Castle Point. It is said that on the return of Hudson from his explorations up the Hudson, lured by the beauty of the spot, he determined to land and make closer acquaintance with its attractions. Accordingly he cast anchor in Weehawken Bay, and as his vessel was at once surrounded by Indians in their canoes, he made them understand by signs that on the morrow he would visit their chiefs. Whereupon they departed, and commenced great preparations for the reception of the white strangers.

The chiefs arrayed themselves in glossy skins, ornamented with feathers and rare-colored shells, while the women of the tribe were dressed in all their finery, which consisted for the most part of highly colored pliable mats or blankets, made from the finest of rushes, and shell necklaces. Hudson and his crew donned their brightest uniforms, and with well polished weapons, presented a goodly array as they disembarked from their vessel. Great curiosity was manifested by all the Indian women, while the braves, although evidently impressed by the gallant bearing of their visitors, preserved that stolid, indifferent demeanor for which the savage has ever been noted.

After a formal welcome by the chiefs, and a judicious distribution of presents by Hudson, the pipe was passed from mouth to mouth and formality dispensed with. Among the party of Hudson was a young gallant, formerly attached to the English court, but who, influenced by his love of adventure, had cast in his lot with the discoverers. He was conspicuous by reason of his great stature and comely appearance, and noting in the daughter of the chief, who was eyeing him furtively, a person of uncommon grace and beauty, he determined to ply the arts that had been so successful at court, and enliven the time by a flirtation with this forest beauty.

He contrived to make her understand what great havoc she had created with his affections, and soon they were familiarly conversing with signs, which were interpreted the more easily through that innate sympathy which is common alike to the maiden of the forest and the belle of the drawing-room. They wandered away through the forest shades, and soon reached a secluded spot on the shore, where they sat down side by side on a fallen log, she reclining lightly against his shoulder. But in spite of the peaceful surroundings, the scene was soon to be changed. One of the warriors, who had long wooed the Indian maiden, and was only waiting to secure sufficient wealth to exchange for her with her father—the old chief—had watched the advances of the bold gallant with a jealous eye, and stealthily followed them through the forest's depths.

His savage nature could not calmly submit to be thus thrust aside for this bold stranger, and as he noted the caresses with which the latter punctuated his sign language, he became inflamed with hate, and several times raised his bow in readiness to send on its mission the deadly arrow, but as often relaxed his effort. But when he saw the maiden almost reclining in the embrace of the stranger, his anger became so fierce, that, maddened beyond restraint, he drew the bow to its utmost tension, and let fly the fatal arrow with so sure an aim that it not only pierced the body of the maiden, but inflicted a mortal wound on the gallant. With features convulsed with jealous anger and rage, he rushed forward to find the maiden's lifeblood gushing forth in streams, and her suitor with agony depicted on his features, endeavoring to stanch the wound in his own breast. Seeing the approach of the savage, he gaspingly pleaded for his life, but of no avail. With demoniacal laughter the crushing blow descended, and man and maiden both lay in the embrace of death at the feet of the infuriated savage. Suddenly seizing the body of the maiden, he bore it on his shoulders, and laid it at the feet of the old chieftain, indicating that her death was caused by the white men whom he was then entertaining.

The fiery, untamed nature of the savage burst forth, and threatening glances were cast upon Hudson and his men. They soon saw that instant flight alone could save their lives from the now thoroughly aroused Indians, and an immediate retreat was ordered. The savages pressed them closely, but by keeping in close array, with blunderbusses ready for action, they were able to reach their boats in safety, and were soon pulled to their vessel. They here missed their companion, but as the shades of night were drawing on, determined that nothing could be done until morning.

At the early dawn of the following day the shrill warwhoop of the Indians was heard, and on looking forth, their uncertainty as to the young man's fate was dispelled, for, circling the vessel in his bark canoe was a savage in full war-paint, brandishing the yellow scalp lock of their companion. So threatening did the aspect of the Indians become, that Hudson immediately weighed anchor and departed from so dangerous a neighborhood.

For over twenty years Hoboken was the home of the New York Yacht Club, which was founded in 1844 by John C. Stevens. The first meeting was held on board his schooner yacht, the *Gimcrack*. In response to his invitation, nine gentlemen appeared and organized what is now one of the most celebrated yacht clubs in the world. In 1845, the first club house was built in the "Elysian Fields," and this continued to be the club's home until 1868, when its headquarters was transferred to Staten Island.

In the early days Hoboken was, like its neighboring city, at times surrounded by water, the high ground terminating at Castle Point forming an island. An old description states: "Hoboken is an island, the westerly side of which is one-half mile from the New Jersey Shore." This space has since been filled in by natural and artificial means, so that the old creek and marshes by which it was surrounded have almost entirely disappeared.

WEEHAWKEN DUELLING GROUND.
WHERE BURR AND HAMILTON FOUGHT. 1801

Above Weehawken and just south of the West shore ferry landing, is the site of the famous duelling ground, specially noted as the spot where the lamented and scholarly Hamilton met his untimely end at the hands of the polished and courtly, yet infamous Burr. About twenty feet above the surface of the water that laves the foot of the overhanging cliffs was a small grassy plateau, about sixty by one hundred feet in area, completely shut off from the surrounding country by perpendicular cliffs reaching up on the sides and back. These in summer were covered with a profusion of vines and mosses, and with the broad river below glittering in quiet ripples, and a rampart of cedar and other bushes at the edge that screened it from the gaze of any casual passer by, it was a spot of unusual beauty, suggesting a peace and quietness, utterly at variance with the bloody deeds there enacted.

And yet its very retirement, rendering it safe from unwelcome intrusion and difficult of access, it being reached only by a rough narrow path from the water, made it a resort for the vengeful and lawless. A long list might be published of those who came to this spot, determined to settle their differences according to the so called "Code of Honor;" but none was so universally regretted as the unfortunate Hamilton, who in a moment of weakness, allowed himself to become the victim of vindictive passions. The march of improvements, necessitating the cutting away of the river bank for railroad purposes, has completely obliterated the spot, but the monument erected thereon to commemorate the place, was moved to the top of the bluff directly back of its original location.

The original Hoboken ferry was established in

DUELLING GROUNDS AT PRESENT TIME.

1774, and like its fellows of that time, was of primitive construction, consisting of row and sail boats. , In 1811, John Stevens applied steam; but this apparently was considered too expensive a method of propulsion, and was superseded by the use of horse-boats, as appears from the following extract from a memorial which he presented March 12, 1814, to the municipal authorities of New York: "That your memoralist hath constructed a boat to be propelled by horses, or mules, which he contemplates to use on the ferry from the foot of Vesey Street to Hoboken, which he hopes will prove a substitute for a steamboat."

This boat seems to have been constructed on a somewhat different plan from those in use on the Paulus Hook ferry. "It had a circular platform in the center, with cleats to give the horses foothold, and the shaft of the paddlewheel was made to revolve by means of cranks on a small wheel on either side of the shaft, geared to a large wheel, on an upright spindle like a crab or cider mill, with two or four arms extending over the platform, and to these arms two, four or eight horses or mules were hitched."

In 1807, an event occurred which excited profound interest. Great crowds gathered along the shores of the Hudson, to witness the departure of a boat up the river, that was to defy wind and current. It was called the *Clermont*, and was built under the superintendence of Robert Fulton. The following advertisement appeared in the *Albany Gazette* of that date:

"The North River Steam Boat will leave Paulus Hook (Jersey City), on Friday the 4th of September, at nine o'clock in the evening. Provisions, good berths, and accommodation are provided. The charge to each passenger is as follows:

"Newburgh,   fare $3,   time 14 hours.
Po'keepsie,   " $4,   " 17 "
Esopus,   " $5,   " 20 "
Hudson,   " $5½,   " 30 "
Albany,   " $7,   " 36 " "

The dimensions of this boat were: length, 100 feet; width, 12 feet; depth, 7 feet.

Chapter LII.

TRADITIONS AND REMINISCENCES.

But the domestic and familiar life of "Old Bergen" possesses an interest beyond that of mere personal associations. The habits and customs of the Fatherland were here transplanted, and the tenacity with which the early settlers clung to them is illustrative of the peculiar steadfastness that is so characteristic of the Dutch temperament. From the Zabriskies on the north to the Van Buskirks on the extreme south, the whole territory was interspersed with the Newkirks, Van Winkles, Van Wagenens, Van Reypens, Brinkerhoffs, Posts, Vreelands and Van Hornes, the last two being very much in evidence.

These families formed a community of their own. They were easy-going folk, satisfied to follow the sun in its rising and its going down. Bound together not only by a community of interest, but oftentimes by ties of consanguinity, there was a kindly feeling, a warm-hearted sympathy, that could not exist under our changed conditions. The early settlers were simple in their wants and habits, and clung religiously to their old associations. They were slow to form new acquaintances, but were firm in their friendships; and whatever local or individual differences might arise, the whole community combined and acted under one impulse when the common interest was involved. Such to a marked degree were the traits displayed by the inhabitants of " Old Bergen."

In a community where the acquaintanceship extends back through a long series of years, and where also a general knowledge is handed down through generations, there is an intimacy and kindly feeling generated that could not be produced in this changing cosmopolitan age. The long, close knowledge of wants and conditions, interwoven with kindly acts and practical sympathy given and received, bound the whole neighborhood in the closest ties, so that they seemed as one unbroken family; the sorrows and afflictions, the trials and perplexities, as well as the joys and happiness, were as common property, and were participated in by all.

When death invaded a family circle, there was a general sadness and outpouring of practical sympathy to those immediately bereaved, and loving hands performed the sad services for the sorrowing. All joined in the simple funeral services and followed on foot the coffin borne on the shoulders of the nearest friends or relatives to its last resting place in the old graveyard, where rest the ashes of so many of our loved ones. The dominie and the doctor usually headed the procession, both wearing over the left shoulder a wide white linen scarf.

The weddings were then as now matters of great interest, and regarded with becoming attention, yet they were tinged with the good practical sense that forbade wastefulness, or dissipation to an unwonted extent. The bride and groom engaged in their ordinary occupations until near the hour for the ceremony, when, arraying themselves in whatever finery they possessed, they submitted to the ordeal with becoming resignation. After the ceremony, the festivities and feasting were indulged in at the house of the bride, and were continued the following day at the house of the bridegroom, after which the young couple were ready to settle down to the practical affairs of life, each anxious and willing to meet the responsibilities of the novel position.

Of course, under the then existing conditions, social intercourse and functions were limited, and very informal. There was a hard, practical side to life that does not exist in these days of countless conveniences; house-keeping then meant actual personal work, and most of the accomplishments taught the young society belle of the day were in the line of useful labor. The skill and ingenuity of the more modern brain had not then furnished the labor saving machines that in these times divest home life of many of the hardships common to the olden time, and the daily duties of the family circle demanded an economical use of every passing hour. Social functions in their present meaning were unknown, and such as were indulged in were combined with, and adapted to the existing domestic conditions. The general helpful spirit that prevailed prevented the existence of many of the anxieties and burdens so common to our social life; each guest became a host and the dreadful fear of some impending breach of etiquette thereby avoided.

In those early days there was a division of labor in all branches of domestic econony, as well as in the rougher out-door work. Quilting bees and meetings for cutting and sewing carpet rags for the much-prized and gaudy floor covering, were joined in by the women, with the same general interest as harvesting or killing times or house raisings were indulged in by the men, and the winter afternoons and evenings were fixed on in advance, so that each in turn might secure the benefit of the general help. Their usual recreations were confined to the neighborly "running in" to gossip on domestic affairs or mayhap to relieve the weary watcher at the bed side of the sick, and the more formal afternoon gatherings or quilting bees, to which shortly after midday, each good dame could be seen wending her way, clad in kerchief and cap, while suspended from her waist was the capacious outside pocket containing a complete outfit for the prudent housewife, with the ball of yarn from which she knitted as she trudged along. These were indeed a welcome relief from the monotonous routine of the daily life, and the bustling dames, as they gathered at the appointed place, were gladly welcomed. With tongues that vied with their clicking needles, they discussed church matters, or, seated about the quilting frame, tracing the intricacies of the gorgeous "Fox Chase" or the solitary "Toad in the puddle," they reconciled all neighborhood differences.

And then the social teas in winter were looked forward to with plesant anticipations, at which perhaps a half dozen congenial couples enjoyed their weekly frolic after the labors of the day were completed. Each couple gave a tea in turn and they would meet at six o'clock, and rarely delayed their departure after ten. The interval was devoted to the enjoyment of the good things of this earth, prepared as only the Dutch housewife knew how, in utter violation of all the known rules of gastronomy or hygiene and with a result that proved all theories at fault. Such were the ordinary recreations of the staid married folk, who knew how to accept the blessings of this life in a becoming manner. Of course there was the periodical donation party or church fair, which awakened a transient excitement in the community, and the various holidays brought each its own peculiar enjoyments.

The annual church picnic was eagerly looked forward to by young and old, and its delights anticipated for weeks before the appointed time. As has been already stated, the church had an abiding place in the hearts of the people, and consequently the whole community was stirred whenever it determined upon any course of action. When the picnic day was fixed, preparations were entered upon that would insure the greatest amount of enjoyment, and were commensurate with the importance of the occasion. The night previous, the skies were eagerly scanned for premonitions of the weather, and the best bib and tucker laid out, which for the fair sex, of course, included colored ribbons and ruffled and embroidered dresses. At the appointed time the rustic beaus and belles wended their way to the church, whither the youngsters had preceded them, while the fathers and mothers, of a more practical turn of mind, finished packing the baskets with "goodies" of every description; and when the start was finally made, the old folks were so fully imbued with the spirit of the occasion that they were just as ready to surrender themselves to the delights of the day as the most enthusiastic of the little ones.

Wagons were lined up and packed so systematically that, in order to unload at all, it was necessary to exactly reverse the order of loading. As soon as all was ready, at the sound of a horn, a score or more of wagons started in a long line, with flags waving, children shouting, dust flying, all bent on crowding as much enjoyment as possible into the one day. Currie's Woods, located just south of the Morris Canal, and between the Old Road and Newark Bay, was always the objective point. In those days there were no groves, with dancing pavilions and variegated smells, but just plain, old-fashioned country woods, carpeted with nature's handiwork, with shady walks and nooks, and redolent with the perfumes distilled in nature's laboratory.

After the occupants of the wagons had been extricated from the same, there was a general scattering; the children, to explore the hidden recesses of the woods, or look for shells on the shore of the Back Bay; the older people, to busy themselves in the preparation of the picnic lunch, while the young men and maidens, impelled by some mysterious law, paired off and wandered away, oftentimes to be seen no more until recalled by the sounding horns for return. The day passed all too quickly; and when the shadows lengthened, the packing was repeated, and the whole concourse wended its way homeward, a tired, happy, dusty, rollicking lot of good old-fashioned Dutchmen, with friendships strengthened, burdens lightened, all stronger and better for the close, informal intercourse that marked the innocent enjoyment of the day.

Chapter LIV.

TRADITIONS AND REMINISCENCES, CONTINUED.

PAUSE and Pfingster were essentially Dutch institutions. On the one the coloring and cracking of eggs were indulged in with as much zest as are the Easter festivities at the White House at the present day; while on Pfingster congenial couples might be seen riding and driving in every direction, oftentimes settling the most momentous affairs of life ere their return.

The Fourth of July was celebrated with special enthusiasm in the olden time, for the memories of Revolutionary struggles and hardships were so recent that the lustre of heroic deeds was yet undimmed. Its observance indicated that it was then invested with a deeper significance than in these latter days. Instead of being given up to noise and merry making, the occasion was arranged so as to fasten in the mind the patriotism of the forefathers, their sufferings and privations, and the necessity of holding fast to their faith and doctrines, in order to insure the perpetuity of the Union.

Early in the day was seen and heard the bustle of preparation. A large tent was erected, and at an early hour the gathering began. They came singly, by families, and by wagon loads, until nearly all the population was gathered within the confines of the parsonage orchard, before alluded to. Tables were spread, and fairly groaned under the abundance of good things, prepared in accordance with the well tested rules of the good old Dutch housewife. The Declaration of Independence was first read, a suitable address was then delivered by the dominie or some other prominent person, and patriotic songs were sung by the Sunday School children. In this way was emphasized the importance of a strict adherence to the principles of Liberty and Justice. As an evidence of the enthusiasm with which the anniversary of our independence was celebrated in the early days, we have the following extract from *The Sentinel of Freedom* of July 28, 1812:

"The farmers of Bergen, being informed that Capt. Decatur would pay them a visit from Newark on the morning of the Anniversary of our Liberty, with his Flying Artillery, and a troop of horse, on his way to New York, made preparations to receive him right royally; but having waited in vain until eleven p. m., it was unanimously agreed to prepare cartridges, man a gun, and proceed to the City of Jersey to fire a salute. Everything being ready by three-quarters past eleven, the party set out, and returned in twenty minutes, although having the misfortune to lose a linch pin, and break one of the axle-trees of the carriage on the road thither."

The following program shows how the Fourth was observed at a somewhat later date:

"OLD BERGEN."

A PUBLISHED
PROGRAM FOR THE CELEBRATION OF THE
4TH OF JULY, 1835.

1. National salute fired at Bergen, and Ringing of Bells.
2. Procession form at 10 o'clock precisely, at the upper Flag Staff, Bergen, and proceed to the church in following order:

OFFICERS OF THE DAY.

Artillery,   Military,   Band.

BEARERS OF LIBERTY CAP AND STANDARD.

Heroes of '76 and Banner.
Orator and Reader.   Rev. Clergy.

CORPORATION OF BERGEN AND JERSEY CITY.

Civic Authorities.
Com. Arrangements.
Citizens in general.

ORDER OF EXERCISES AT CHURCH.

Prayer. .   Ode.
Declaration of Independence.
Music by Band.   Oration.
Ode.   Music by Band.
Benediction.

Preserve the same order from church, and proceed to the Square, where a National salute will be fired. Then proceed to Five Corners, dismiss and Dine.

The annual training day, when all able-bodied men were compelled to muster for enrollment and drill, was an occasion very generally recognized and gathered a most wonderful aggregation of armed warriors. At Christmas time Santa Claus was eagerly welcomed, and gifts were exchanged, the value of which was estimated not from a monetary standpoint, but because of the wealth of love and affection they represented.

But New Year's Day was the crowning event of the year, and was celebrated by all. Calls were interchanged and friendships renewed in the social manner peculiar to those days, and from early morn until sometimes the dawning of the next day, the cordial greetings were given and received. On every New Year's Day, the Dominie made special addresses to the different classes of the congregation—the old, the middle-aged, and the young; and in turn each stood as indicated. The fathers in Israel, with whitened heads and bent and tottering forms, listened to the words of love and encouragement from their revered pastor, as he assured them of his love and sympathy, and, commending them for their steadfastness, reminded them of the reward of the faithful. They were followed by the middle-aged, those who were in the full vigor of manhood; these he earnestly besought to bear the heat and burden of the day, and with wise and appropriate words, strengthened them in the faith. Lastly the young, so closely enwrapped in his affections, hung upon the kindly words spoken to them, as though his great love for them, impelled the going out to him of their young hearts, cheering and helping them by his loving admonitions and advice.

Chapter LV.

TRADITIONS AND REMINISCENCES, CONTINUED.

THE amusements of the young from their very simplicity, were the more enjoyable. The young ladies' constitutions in those days did not require expensive theatre parties and late suppers to revive their failing energies. When an outing was determined upon, the young man appeared on horseback, and halting at the mounting block, one of which adorned every front entrance, awaited the appearance of his maid, who mounted upon the pillion behind him and, prompted by a very proper Dutch timidity, clasped him convulsively about the waist to ensure herself against falling. They ambled along the leafy paths and shady roads, returning with an appetite that enabled them to do full justice to the bountiful meal awaiting them.

This horseback riding was followed by the more exclusive buggy, and long lines of these easy-riding vehicles, wending their way in the evening in every direction, testified to their popularity. Often a stop would be made at some convenient hostelry, where, under the inspiration of the negro fiddler, the hours were all too quickly consumed in the delights of the fascinating schottische, the stately quadrille, or the more rollicking Virginian reel. Oh! the delights of those moonlight rides through the shady back road, not a sound to be heard save the rustling of the shimmering leaves and the katydid's chirp, as the horse ambled softly along, guided by fair hands—for the girls insisted on driving when the woods came in

CIDER PRESS

sight, and the intelligent animal softened his gait to a slow walk, as if to express his intense sympathy.

Again, at the proper seasons, picnics, straw-rides and sleigh-rides were indulged in, and the absence of formality, and the consciousness that all were possessed of a sincere spirit of friendliness, made them most enjoyable.

In winter at the first indication of sufficient snow, the girls were notified, wagon boxes were placed on runners and filled with sweet, well-cured salt hay or straw, and an abundance of buffalo robes furnished. In the early evening hour the favored ones were called for, and to the music of silvery voices and resonant sleigh bells, the distance to Bergen Point or Hackensack was soon covered and the remaining hours devoted to that superlative enjoyment that can be fully appreciated only through realization. The names of Wauters and Pennoyer are so thoroughly identified with good substantial suppers and terpsichorean exercise that their mere mention opens up the vista of the past and brings again to view the scene in all its vivid freshness.

Along what was called Back Lane, now West Side Avenue, were melon patches and a peach orchard, possessing great attraction for the youth of the day, especially as there were cedar woods hard by, whose low, bushy branches afforded a convenient place of refuge from the eyes of the sometimes too inquisitive owners.

Probably the most attractive place in the old town at a certain season of the year was Van Wagenen's cider press (near where his house now stands), about which the boys clustered like flies around a molasses barrel; and no wonder, for no more exquisite enjoyment could be devised than a judicious combination of a well selected straw and an overflowing cider barrel. Jove never sipped more delicious nectar, than the new cider, wrapping as it did the senses in a most ecstatic dream, and obliterating all idea of present or future responsibility.

Near by could be seen, on warm, sunny days, the portly form of "Old Uncle Gatty," seated in the midst of his beehives, calmly smoking his old clay pipe, blackened by long use, and watching his industrious workers as they piled up their wealth of sweetness. Although ignorant, perhaps, of what might be termed scientific bee lore, his knowledge of the habits of the little insects was verified by the seeming affection with which they encircled him, buzzing about his head as though trying to inform him of the discovery of some new, honey-laden flower, or lingering for a moment for his words of praise and encouragement. He talked with them as though he considered them possessed of human intelligence, and whenever any one exhibited unusual stupidity, his favorite comparison, spoken in the Dutch vernacular, was: "Huh! you don't know half as much as one of my bees!"

The harvesting was carried on by an interchange of services, and the "killing time" (which always came after cold weather had set in), when the well nurtured hogs and beeves were deftly despatched to their happy grazing fields, was oftentimes made an occasion of great jollification. The farmers arranged to assist each other, so that the labor was lightened, and, with few exceptions, the work of the day finished by mid-afternoon. After refreshments, "weight guessing" was indulged in, while the sedative pipe quieted the nerves of those who had become unduly excited, and prepared them for a like experience at some neighboring farm the following day. The young people always longed eagerly for this time, when the old kitchen became redolent with savory smells, and the manufacture of sausage, roelechas, head cheese and, last but not least, the aromatic mince meat, suggested possibilities scarcely realized in an Epicurean dream.

The skins of the cattle killed were sent to the tannery, the proprietor of which exacted as toll one-half the quantity tanned. The leather returned to the farmer was laid aside to await the periodical visit of the shoemaker, whose custom was to travel from house to house, in order to make or cobble the shoes of the family.

Another industry in the fall was the collecting of honey from the beehives, which were to be found near every well regulated farm house ; and lucky was the youngster who received permission to participate in this work. There was something so fascinating in the thought of being wakened in the early morning hours and groping through the gloom to the kitchen, where the flickering light of the fire only disclosed the shadows and dark recesses of the room, thereby increasing the chills that made the teeth clatter like castanets, not to be dispelled until after the disappearance of a bowl of hot supporn. Then, each person being provided with the ever-present woolen comforter closely wrapped about the neck and head, with a mysterious air and stealthy tread, in true keeping with the nefarious deed about to be performed, the expedition started, and it was an experience never to be forgotten.

The honey could be collected with comparative safety in the early morning, when the crisp, cold air had benumbed the active little denizens of the hive, and rendered them unable to use their natural means of defense in resisting the attack upon their stores of wealth. Preparations were made the night before by wrapping pine splints with cotton cloth and dipping them in melted brimstone. In the morning these were lighted and placed beneath the hives, and the fumes so stupified the bees that the plunderers were enabled to select at will such combs of honey as seemed to them judicious. Usually sufficient store was left to afford the bees a meagre sustenance until the return of the spring sunshine again tempted them forth in search of their natural food, but frequently the whole hive was denuded and the bee family destroyed.

Often in the early morning hour could be heard the deep bay of the fox hound echoing over the fields, as, urged by his revengeful master, he swiftly and unerringly tracked the midnight marauder, through whose shrewd cunning the poultry yard had been depleted.

Chapter LVI.

CUSTOMS AND HABITS.

During the winter months the young people likewise enjoyed candle making. In those early days as a rule, lard lamps and tallow dips were used for illuminating purposes, but sometimes clam shells were filled with melted lard in which a piece of cotton cloth was inserted, and the oil being then allowed to harden, the shell lamps were laid aside for future use. When needed, the wick was lighted, and the heat from its flame kept sufficient of the surrounding lard melted to ensure a continuous feeding, thus furnishing a somewhat dim and flickering light.

The tallow dips, requiring no special expense, were in very general use, and were made as follows: Cotton wicks were cut in the required lengths, and hung in the middle over a rounded stick, which was sufficiently long to accommodate twelve or fifteen of them. When a number of these had been prepared, they were in turn plunged into a vessel of melted tallow, and when encrusted with the grease, were withdrawn and placed upon a frame to cool and harden. This process was repeated frequently, and as the candles grew larger with each dipping, they soon became the required size, when they were hung in the garrets for use as needed.

After the emancipation of the slaves, so attached had they become to their masters, that many of them absolutely refused to accept their freedom in the sense of self dependence, always regarding themselves as part and parcel of the old home. Some of them, addicted to the roving, careless life that seems to have been transmitted to them from some far-off ancestor, roamed with their descendants through the woods and swamps in search of blackberries, huckleberries, or the "snapping turtle," which, under proper manipulation, was considered a choice and dainty dish, rivalling in toothsomeness the terrapin of the South; while others devoted their energies to the capture of the frost fish or "killies" that at certain seasons swarmed in the Hackensack River and the neighboring marshes. Mushrooms abounded in the fields, and were sought after during the early morning hours by others of the black folk, and the appearance of the "Rovers" with a full supply at the "back kitchen" door was hailed with delight. Others again engaged in business transactions. The sonorous and melodious voice of "Old Yon" as he cried "fresh buttermilk," carried in the same churn from which the butter had been taken, was familiar to all, while "Lame Tomachy," with his solitary ox, warranted sound and kind in double or single harness, was an unique figure in the early days. "Old Betty's" chickens and eggs possessed a peculiarly appetizing flavor, and her culinary accomplishments were especially appreciated by the younger generation when carried by their wanderings beyond the dinner hour of the home.

All throughout the territory bounded by the meadows, from Bergen Point to the northern limit, were to be found nut-bearing trees, their fruit being highly prized for household use. The cool, crisp air of early winter was eagerly longed for, and at the first indication of frost, expeditions were organized to gather the nuts that had been rudely shaken from their downy beds by the wintry blasts. Hickory nuts and chestnuts were the most abundant, the trees growing in groups; and many of these were regarded, by a sort of unwritten law, as the special property of different coteries of boys, usually of those living in their immediate neighborhood. Sometimes this custom was infringed upon by the more lawless, and fierce fights resulted, during which the poles intended for knocking down the nuts were employed by the rival bands in knocking down their opponents. This was, however, only an occasional experience, as the right of " preëmption " was generally recognized.

In various parts of the territory were scattered black walnut trees, many of which were left standing for ornament or shade, after the clearing away of all the others; and their leafless branches studded with clusters of black balls tossing against the wintry sky, formed a unique feature of the landscape. These walnuts were, however, avoided by the more fastidious, as their gathering imparted an almost indelible stain to the hands, that could be obliterated only after persistent effort.

A favorite custom of the boys during the fall months, was to gather on Saturdays in " The Cedars," where, with the combined plunder gathered throughout the week, in the shape of eggs, coffee, or whatever material in the culinary line that could be secured, they would imitate the feasts indulged in by Marion and his men. Sometimes, the rations thus collected being inadequate, surreptitious visits were made to the neighboring fields and their products confiscated. Tubers were so artistically separated from the sweet potato vines by burrowing under the side hills, that the sparseness of the crop at harvest time suggested to the owner the wisdom of discontinuing their cultivation.

After these feasts, the cooking utensils were again secreted in their accustomed hiding places, and then hunting for hornets' nests was sometimes indulged in. When a nest was discovered, the boys' experience taught them to institute an elaborate and carefully considered plan of attack. Ammunition, in the shape of well selected stones, was gathered, branches of cedar trees suitable for defence were conveniently placed and the bearings of the nearest ditch carefully studied. This latter was a precautionary measure that was taken advantage of only in the direst extremity. The common belief being that an angry hornet would dart toward the spot from which a stone was thrown, a simultaneous attack from different points, was usually determined on, so that the hornets' idea of locality might be somewhat confused, and thus afford an opportunity of escape to the attacking party. At a given signal the plan was carried out; at the first jostling of the nest, out poured the enraged insects in swarms, and away scampered the marauders in every direction in their endeavors to escape from the wrath to come. Sometimes an agonized shriek, accompanied by a frenzied waving of branches, would indicate that some infuriated insect had inserted his business end under the coat collar of his victim, and was plying his art with all the vigor of which it was capable. At about this period of time the location of the ditch was eagerly sought after, and the fun was over.

Chapter LVII.

THE OLD HOMES.

The houses of the olden times were low, one-story buildings, with peaked roof, facing and along the line of the street, with a wide hall running through the middle of the house and closed at the front with a divided door. This door was shaded by a small porch with side seats, a most convenient place for the assembling of neighbors, when making friendly calls or discussing any matters of general interest. There are very few houses of the old type remaining, and these have been so changed and modernized that the old homes are not what they used to be.

The wide hall was in the summer time the living room of the family, and here could be found the busy housewife, with carding or spinning wheel, adding to her household stores, and ever and anon touching with her foot the great mahogany rocker that had soothed the restlessness of former generations, while the old grandmother sat nodding and dozing in her easy chair, or teaching the youngsters the mysteries of patchwork, or narrowing down the stocking heel, or perhaps guiding the clumsy fingers over the artistic and much-prized sampler.

The old patriarch of the family sat near-by, dandling

on his knee mayhap the great-grandchild, to the rhythmical cadence of:—

OLD HOME.

"Trippe trop a tronches, Varkes in the vonches,
Couches in the clawver, Pearches in the hawver,
Calfes in the long a gras, Anches in the wasser plos,
And the clina young-a, so groat wass."

Grandfather's clock ticked noisily in the corner, with Luna's fair face peeping over the dial and marking the quarters with a shameless irregularity, while the upper half-door stood hospitably open as if inviting the passer-by to join in the friendly chat or harmless gossip.

Opening into the hall were the sleeping rooms on the one side, and the parlor on the other, the latter seldom opened, except in case of marriage or death, or for the periodical cleaning, when after a thorough sweeping and dusting, it was again closed until some special ceremony required its opening. Sometimes in the rear of the parlor was the guest chamber, with its high-post bedstead, draped and festooned with highly colored valances, profusely fringed. The warming pan stood in the corner, and was a most welcome adjunct in those days of frigid rooms; for, filled with hot embers from the kitchen fire, it was passed between the icy sheets, imparting a delightful warmth that was most grateful to the half-frozen guest, as with acrobatic feat, he plunged into the billowy feather bed and— disappeared.

But the glory of the old home was the kitchen, with its great fire-place, laughing with wide-open hospitality, extending across the entire width, with immense chimneys, in which the meats were sometimes smoked; the great back-log sputtered with its pungent smoke curling lazily upward, flanked and overhung with pot-hooks and trammels, suspending over the fire the pots and kettles which simmered with the noon-day meal; and on the side was the pot of supporn, with dish and spoon always ready for the hungry wayfarer, or whoever chose to partake.

Near by the cavernous oven gaped yawningly, as if eager to swallow the luscious pies and cakes prepared by the good housewife as her weekly contributions towards the domestic economy. Sometimes the neighbors gathered with the family on some stormy afternoon, and plates of rosy-cheeked apples and toothsome nuts, washed down with copious draughts of cider, increased the comfort and good cheer. And then what an inviting place the kitchen was on winter evenings for the family gathering, while oftentimes the wail of the Storm King about the wide chimney tops formed a weird accompaniment to the evening hymns so often sung; or perhaps at nightfall the little ones were gathered about the mother's knee, and by the fitful blaze of the wood fire or flickering candle flame, the Bible stories from scenes depicted on the tiling about the fire place were told.

Nor must the great garret, extending over the whole house, with its nooks, and corners, peopled with the shadowy forms of long ago, be forgotten. This was indeed the store-house of the family. Piles of apples and nuts occupied the corners, and from the rafters were festooned strings of red peppers, clusters of seed corn, and bunches of dried herbs, filling the air with their spicy aroma, while tables bearing dozens of mince and pumpkin pies were overhung with strings of sausage.

At the end of the house was the home garden, usually superintended by the auntie, which was filled with a profusion of old-fashioned *blumechas;* four o'clocks and tulips, ragged sailors and poppies, banked with the blooming peony and stately dahlia, with the sweet-smelling syringa and lilac in the background, while the ever-present boxtree lent a sombre shade to the coloring. The fragrant mint and sweet marjoram, the savory sage, the pungent thyme, and the soothing lavender, mingled their odors in the air, the memory of which turns back the wheels of time and blots out all the intervening years.

The furniture was chosen and designed for its fitness and durability, the truth of which is proven by the fact that although made more than two centuries ago, there are specimens of this furniture gracing the drawing-rooms of the present day in a better state of preservation than articles of much more modern manufacture. Everything was kept scrupulously clean, and the good housewife displayed with pride the shining array of pots and pans upon her kitchen dressers, while the well scrubbed floor, ornamented in the early days with the strip of bright-colored carpet, was an object of housewifely pride.

Chapter LVIII.

CUSTOMS.

THE lack of facilities for manufacture of clothing or household goods impelled the frugal and self-respecting to habits of industry, and the whir of the spinning wheel was heard whenever a few minutes relief from housekeeping duties allowed. The girls were early taught the mysteries of spinning, weaving, and knitting, and the well stored chest of the youthful bride gave abundant evidence of her own industrious habits. Not only were the garments home spun; but the warp and woof were made from the flax grown in the home field and the wool shorn from the well kept sheep; and in some old families, are still found blankets and bedding, the handiwork of the great grandmothers in their early days.

Owing to the primitive condition of the times, many industries now unknown in household economy were then engaged in, and as a consequence actual labor necessary to be performed forbade idleness on the part of the enterprising householder. The spices for home use were often crushed by means of two stones, one being hollowed out to receive the whole berry, and the other, of suitable size and shape, being used for pounding. These were substituted in the homes of the well-to-do, by a mortar and pestle, made of metal, specimens of which are still shown with pride by the descendants of the early settlers. Mustard seed was crushed by placing a quantity of it in a round bottomed iron pot, and on it, a medium sized cannon ball. This pot was taken on the lap, and by imparting to it a rotary motion, the seed was crushed, and the operator bathed in copious tears from the effect of the pungent odor.

The churning was usually done by hand. In some cases large platform wheels were erected in the cellar at an incline, and by means of strips of wood nailed just within the rim, a circular walk was formed. On this dogs were placed, and as they proceeded on their endless journey, the wheel was made to revolve. This was connected with the dasher by means of projecting arms, and the churning accomplished in a comparatively easy manner to all—except the dogs. Sometimes the old ram of the flock was utilized, but the futility of his efforts to reach the end of his journey, seemingly soured his disposition to such a degree of pugnacity, that in a short time, he was subjected to the butcher's knife, and in the shape of nutritive mutton—the quality of which was strengthened by the unwonted exercise in which he was compelled to indulge—became the foundation for unexceptionable broth.

The Dutch language prevailed almost exclusively to within the last half century, especially in the intercourse of the inhabitants with each other; and even after the church services were regularly held in English, the occasional Sunday afternoon preaching in

Dutch was hailed with great satisfaction and rejoicing by the older people of the congregation.

But the old days with their conservative progressiveness are gone never to return. We are facing a new era, and events crowd each other so rapidly that we scarce catch a glimpse of their departing shadows. New customs and associations environ us; and yet, like the traveller, who at eventide standing on some eminence, looks back over the surrounding landscape, and catches only the sun-tipped peaks of the mountain heights, the while forgetting the shadowy nooks and rugged cliffs, the rills and dashing waterfalls, that lend completeness to the picture; so as we indulge in retrospect, we are apt to recall only the gilded experiences of the past, forgetting the humdrum, everyday life that went so far to make up the days and years that have long passed away.

It is to be hoped that the historic importance of "Old Bergen" may in the near future be recognized, and that a "New Bergen" may spring up, and under that name not only gain the whole of its old possessions, but also include under its government the, to be one day, densely populated territory reaching out to and beyond the green hills of the Oranges.

Already its future prominence is foreshadowed, and financial and commercial interests are clustering here that will ere long rival in magnitude and importance even the enterprises of the great city of which it has so long been a neighbor.

THE END.

Index

----, Aunt Rachel 268 Dick 270 Garret 239 George 129 John the Laugher 30 Lame Tomachy 308 Old Betty 308 Old Dominie 185 Old Yon 308 Sal 270 William the Testy 70
ABEEL, Dr 279 Rev Dr 278
ABRAHAM, Cornelis 77
ADRIAENSEN, Maryn 44
ADRIENSE, Lawrence 249
ALDRIDGE, John 196 Thomas 196
AMERMAN, Dr 185 James L 184
ANDERSON, Ephraim 98
ANDRE, 115-117 Maj 116
ANDROS, Edmund 82
ARENTSE, Claes 77
ARGALLS, Samuel 16
ARNOLD, 115-117 121 Benedict 238
BACHER, Claas Jansen 49
BAKER, Mr 80
BALDWIN, Edmund 197
BANGHART, George 199
BANTA, Siebe Epkse 187
BARKER, Nicholas Jansen 54
BARNUM, P T 274
BARRY, Dr 196 E D 195
BAUMAN, Maj 140
BAYARD, Samuel 276
BENSUM, Matheus 208
BERKELEY, Lord 71
BERRY, Capt 80 John 80
BERTHOLF, G 168
BIENFIELD, Capt 82
BLEECKER, William P 197
BLINKERHOF, Cornelis 209
BLINKERHOFF, Cornelius C 86
BLISS, Elisha Jr 202
BLOCK, 17 Adrian 16
BOGARDUS, Dominie 27 32
BONAR, Jas B 201
BONNELL, Alexander 201-202
BOUT, 30 41 Jan Evertsen 26 30 38-39
BRADFORD, George 23 Gov 23
BRETT, Cornelius 185
BRINKERHOFF, 290 Cornelis 168
BROUWER, Uldrich 209
BROWER, Jacob I 86
BROWN, Capt 250 Tom 249
BURR, 286
BUSH, Garret 251
BUSKIRK, 128 Maj 127
CABOT, 9 67 John 3 10 Sebastian 3 10
CAMERON, Simon 243
CAPTAIN, Jans 49
CARSTENSEN, Claas 44
CARTERET, 75 206 George 71 Gov 31 73 80 82 88 249 Philip 71 203 239
CHADEAYNE, Miss 222
CHAMPE, 120-121 John 117 Sgt 118
CHARLES II, King of England 67 73 203
CHRISTAEN, Hendrick 16
CHRISTANSEN, 17
CLAERSEN, Dirck 49

CLAUSEN, Dirck 54
CLINTON, 137-138 Henry 115-116 135-136 138-139
COLFAX, Brig Gen 241
COLUMBUS, 2
COLVE, 82 Anthony 76
COOPER, Mr 151 153 Peter 151
CORNELISEN, Dominie 175 179 John 174 Mr 176 179
CORNELISON, John M 197
CORNWALLIS, 137-140 Lord 105
CORTELYOU, Jacques 54 64
CORTSTIANSEN, Hendrick 16
COS, Claas Petersen Garrabrant 49 Garrabrant 49
COSMAN, Capt 141
CRAIGHEAD, J G 201-202
CROSBY, Mr 202 Orrin H 201 202
CUMMINGS, Gen 257
CURTENIUS, A 168
CUYLER, Col 111 122 135
DE BEVILLE, Gen 137
DECATUR, Capt 298
DEDRICHS, Abraham 172
DE GAMA, Vasco 1
DE LACHER, Jan 230
DEMAREST, Prof 176
DE MOTT, 268 Matheus 209
DEMOTTE, 249
DE SILLE, Nicasius 54
DE VRIES, 32 37 Capt 27
DE WINT, Petrus 171
DEWITT, Gasherie 216
DEY, Anthony 230
DICKINSON, Mr 221 Wm L 221
DIEDERICK, Abraham 85
DIEDRICK, Hans 78
DIGBY, Admiral 139
DOANE, Rt Rev Bishop 196
DONGAN, Thomas 82
DUANE, James 124

DUBOIS, Bishop 197-198 Gualterus 168 Gualtherus 170
DU PORTAIL, Gen 137
DURYEA, Philip 279
DUSENBERRY, Henry 202
EARLE, 161 Peter 160
EDGE, Isaac 254
EDSALL, 79 Mr 82 Samuel 81 Wm Samuel 74
EDWARDS, Lewis A 254
EICKBE, Edward 80
ELIZABETH, Queen of England 20
ELLSWORTH, 223
ERICKSON, R 168
EVERTSEN, Jan 30
FASH, Christopher H 197
FERGUSON, John 141
FITCH, Henry 235
FITJE, 252
FORSYTH, Capt 130 132
FRANKS, J J 161
FREDERICKS, Thomas 77
FREEMAN, B 168
FRELINGHUYSEN, Col 242 J W 242
FRENCH, Edward W 202
FULTON, Robert 286
GAHAGEN, 216
GARRETSON, John 240
GATES, Gen 98
GAUTIER, 249
GEORGE, King of England 174
GEORGE III, King of England 92
GERRABRANTS, Myndert 85
GERREBRANTS, Cornelius K 85
GERRITSE, Gerit 239 Gerrit 77
GIFFORD, George 161
GILLIE, 261-262
GILLIS, Judge 154
GORDON, L J 151
GRANGER, Gen 257 Gideon 257 259
GRAVES, Jared W 196 Miss 222

GREEN, Gen 104
GREENE, Gen 102 104 135
GRIFFITH, David H 196
GUIS, W R 196
HALLOCK, 161
HAMILTON, 286 Alexander 124
HANDY, Capt 129 Levin 130
HARDING, Geo 141 Wm 140
HARRISON, S D 197 Thomas 196
HARTMANS, Maritje 209
HASBROUCK, Dr 222 Washington 222
HAYES, Maj 110-111
HECKEWELDER, John 10
HENDRICKSEN, Jan 240
HICKMAN, Robert 276
HOECK, Paulus 30
HORNBLOWER, Justice 223
HOUSE, Prof 161
HOWE, Gen 95 104 Lord 97 174 William 115 Wm 105
HUDSON, 4 7-10 15 281-284 Henry 3 67
HUNT, 223
INDIAN, Bomokan 49 Job 49 Koghkenningh 49 Memiwokan 49 Saghkow 49 Sames 49 Therincques 49 Wairimus Conwee 49 Wawapehack 49 Wewenatokee 49
IRVING, 69 124 129 Washington 62 236
JACKSON, Dominie 173 John P 156 William 171-172 176
JACOBUS, James 200
JAMES, Thomas 197
JANSEN, Garret 240 Jacob 203 Michael 42 46 54 60 204 Wm 65
JOHNSON, Michael 240
JOHNSTON, Jno 201
JOUET, 7
KADMUS, Dirck 86

KELLY, Father 198 Rev Father 198
KENNEDY, 230
KIEFT, 30-31 35 37-38 40-42 Director 35 Gov 33-34 37 William 29 69
KIERSTED, Sarah 80
KING OF ENGLAND, 103 139
KNICKERBOCKER, Diedrich 252
KNOWLTON, 99 Maj 98
KNYPHAUSEN, Gen 132
KUYPER, Hendricus 172
LABREE, Lawrence 275
LACHER, Jan de 30
LAFAYETTE, 124 133 138 142 264 272-273 Gen 135
LAMBRECHTSEN, 10
LATROBE, H B 151
LAWRENCE, William 82
LEE, 121 124 126-128 130 135 272 Harry 123 Maj 117-118 124-125 129
LEYT, J 168
LINSLEY, Geo H 220 Mr 220-221
LIVINGSTON, Chancellor 277 Gov 104 110-114 Wm 99
LONGSTREET, Aaron 90
LUBBERSE, Jan 209
LUPARDUS, W 168
MAHAN, William 198
MANCIUS, George W 168
MARCELLESSEN, Peter 77
MARINUS, H 168
MARION, 310
MARTIN, Peter 219
MAY, 17 20-21 Cornelius 19 Cornelius Jacobus 16
MCALLISTER, Lt 124
MCBIRNEY, James C 202
MCCLINTOCK, Dr 199
MCCURDY, Archibald 141
MCLANE, Capt 126 129
MEGAPOLENSIS, John 168 Samuel 168

MERCER, 99 103 143 Gen 94-95 102
  106-107 Hugh 93
MERSELES, Jacob M 161 202
MEYNDERTSON, Myndert 31
MICHELSE, Elias 77
MICHIELSE, Johannis 209
MICHIELSEN, Ilias 72
MIDDLETON, Cornet 118
MINUIT, 29 Peter 21
MONTGOMERY, James 196
NEGRO, Sam 270-271
NEWKIRK, 290
NICOLL, 79 Col 81
NICOLLS, Col 71 Mr 80 Richard 70
NIEWWENHUYSEN, Wilhelmus 168
O'CALLAGHAN, 20
OGDEN, Aaron 116 Capt 116 Col 139
  Matthew 139
OLCUTT, Rev Mr 181
OLDEN, Gov 243
PARKER, John G 201-202 Mr 201-202
PAULAZ, Michael 32
PAUW, 28 30 Michael 26
PENHORNE, Mr 80
PENNINGTON, Gov 241
PETERSEN, Claas 49
POST, 290 Adrien 78
POTTER, John W 13
POUWELSIE, Johannis 209
PRINCE OF ORANGE, 20
PUTNAM, F C 197 Gen 98
RAYMOND, John 202
ROBERTSON, 10
ROCHAMBEAU, Count de 137
ROCHEFOUCAULD, Duke de 150
ROOSE, Garret 86
ROSEGRANT, Elijah 211
ROY, Jacob Jacobson 44
RUDDEROW, John 197
RUDOLF, Sgt 39
RUDOLPH, Lt 124

SCOTT, George 80
SEGGELSE, Robert 209
SEKIER, Dirck 49
SELYN, Henry 170 Mr 170
SELYNS, Henricus 168
SICKELS, Abraham 86
SICKELSE, Zacharias 86
SICKLES, Abraham 169
SIGGELS, Hendrick V 86
SIP, Ido I 86 Maritze Aryanse 187
  Siebe Epkse 187
SMEEMAN, Harman 60 72
SMITH, 223 Albert T 220 Michele 80
  Mr 220
SPIER, Hendrich H 86
STEIMMETS, Caspar 72
STEVENS, Col 277 John 234 276 287
  John C 284 Mr 276
STIRLING, Lord 94 126 128
STOCKTON, 153
STOFFLESEN, 41
STOKES, 153
STRAATMAKER, Dirck 31
STUYNHUYSEN, 204 E 203 205-206
  Engelbert 169 187 203 205-206
STUYVESANT, Gov 31 44-45 48 74
  276 Mr 102 P 54 Peter 42
STYNMETS, Caspar 60 78
SUTHERLAND, Maj 125 127
SUTPHEN, Jno S 197
SWIFT, Gen 241
SYCKLES, Robt 172
SYKLES, Abraham 172
TAERS, Arent 86
TAYLOR, Benjamin C 180 Dr 163
  182 184 192 243 Rev Dr 279
TEUNISEN, 41
THOMAS, William 196
THOMASSE, Fredrick 209 Johannis
  209
THROCKMORTON, Barberie 197
TOMPKINS, Gov 241-242

TONNELLE, 271
TYSEN, Lysbet 49
UMPANE, George 81
VAN BENTHUYSEN, P 169
VAN BUREN, Sylvester 217
VAN BUSKIRK, 239 249 290 Andries 86 Jacobus 85 Lereymis 86 Lowrens 86
VANDER DONK, Adrien 9-10
VANDEROFF, Hendrick 86
VAN GIESEN, B 206 Reynier Bastiase 169
VAN HORN, 178
VAN HORNE, 249 253 290 Canal Bridge John 239 Jacob I 86 John 86 239 Johns John 239 Mill Creek John 239 Trinches John 239
VAN HOUTEN, 168 Johannis 86 172
VAN HULST, William 21
VAN NEWKIRK, Cornelius 85
VAN PUTTEN, Aert Teunisen 31
VAN REYPEN, 270 290 Garret D 244
VAN RIPER, 178 217 248
VAN SCHIE, Cornelius 168
VAN TWILLER, Gov 27 Wouter 29
VAN VLECK, Tilman 60
VAN VORST, 28 32 232 C 230 Cornelis 27 30 42 Cornelius 160 253
VAN VORTS, Ide 72
VAN WAGENEN, 178 270 290 303 Johannis 172 Old Uncle Gatty 304
VAN WAGENER, Jacob G 86 Johannis G 86
VAN WAGENING, Garret 239
VAN WAGNER, Jacob G 86
VAN WINKELL, Hendrich 86
VAN WINKLE, 178 290 Daniel 86 172 Jacob 239 Jacob Jacobse 209

VAN WORST, Cornelius 86
VAN ZUREN, Caspar 168 Casper 165
VARICK, Abraham 230
VERLET, Nicholas 72
VERLETT, Nicholas 31 74 276
VERMEULEN, Adrien 169 Andrien 209
VERPLANCK, Abraham Isaacsen 30
VERRAZANO, 9
VIDAL, F P 161
VREELAND, 178 249-250 290 George 172 Michael C 86 Michael Jansen 49
VREELANDT, Johannis 86
WALLINGS, Jacobse 239
WANSEY, Henry 150
WARD, Capt 135 Elizur 197 Maj 109 140-141
WASHINGTON, 93 95 102-106 114-117 123-125 133-134 136-139 142-143 238-239 272-273 Gen 111 113 116 135 268
WAYNE, 123 Brig Gen 111 Gen 111 136
WELSH, James 217 John 217 Schoolmaster 218
WESTERVELT, Richard H 202
WILLIAM HENRY, Prince of ? 139
WILLIAMSEN, Hendrick 240
WILLIAMSON, Gov 272
WILSON, Geo B 176
WINDS, Gen 111
WOUTERSON, 41 Egbert 30 38
WRIGHT, E R 196
WYNKOOP, Robert D 202
YORK, Duke of 67-68 82
ZABRISKIE, 249 290
ZIEKEN, Dirck 44

www.ingramcontent.com/pod-product-compliance
Lightning Source LLC
Chambersburg PA
CBHW051628230426
43669CB00013B/2215